THE FULL GOSPEL

Various Aspects of the Good News

Zac Poonen

The Full Gospel: *Various Aspects of the Good News*

© Zac Poonen, 1996

1 3 5 7 9 10 8 6 4 2

www.cfcindia.com

Paperback ISBN: 9789384302146
ePub ISBN: 9789384302443
Kindle ISBN: 9789384302757

For further details please contact:

Christian Fellowship Church
40 DaCosta Square,
Wheeler Road Extension
Bangalore – 560084
India
email: cfc@cfcindia.com

Contents

1. The Full Gospel 1

2. The Balance of Truth 10

3. Having a Firm Grip on the Christian Life 21

4. The Threefold Exchange at the Cross 28

5. That Which was from the Beginning 39

6. Married to Christ 50

7. How God Exposes Pharisees in the Church 61

8. Faith, Brokenness and Victory 72

9. Are You Serving God or Money? 83

10. Standing in the Gap Before the Lord 94

11. Two Types of Backsliders and Two Types of Leaders 103

12. A Church Triumphant Over Satan 109

13. No Man Can Boast in God's Presence 117

14. Warnings to the Church for the Last Days 127

15. What a Happy Year it will Be 138

16. Will You Shrink Away from the Lord When He Returns? . 147

17. The Influence of One Man 154

18. Learning Gentleness from Jesus 162

19. Your Decisions Determine What You Become 168

20. Satan is the Ruler of Darkness and the Father of Lies ... 173

21. Helping God!! 175

22. The Ministry of Melchizedek 178

23. The Secret of Discernment 181

24. Submission to the Elders of the Church 183

25. A Spiritual Check-Up 186

26. Proving God's Perfect Will 188

1

The Full Gospel

"I did not shrink back from declaring to you the whole purpose of God"
(Acts 20:27).

The apostle Paul spent three years in Ephesus, preaching night and day (*Acts 20:31*). What did he preach?

To the unconverted heathen, he preached repentance towards God and faith in our Lord Jesus Christ (*Acts 20:21*). But to those who had become believers he preached *"the whole purpose of God"* (*Acts 20:27*).

Today, most preachers preach only *"faith"* – and that too a counterfeit one – which has resulted in many spiritual *"miscarriages"* in evangelistic meetings, producing a great multitude of half-converted *"believers"*, who have never turned from their sins, but who want to come to Jesus only in order to be "blessed".

Some preachers however are more Scriptural, and preach that repentance must precede faith – as Paul did.

But Paul did not stop even there. He went on to preach the full gospel of the grace of God (*Acts 20:24*).

Many think that they have experienced the 'full gospel' when they have known Jesus as Saviour AND Baptizer in the Holy Spirit.

But *Hebrews 6:1, 2* tells us this is only the beginning of the Christian life: "*The elementary teachings concerning the Christ – the foundation of repentance and faith* (that is, forgiveness of sins – knowing Jesus as Saviour), *baptisms and laying on of hands* (that is baptism in water and baptism in the Holy Spirit – knowing Jesus as the Baptizer in the Holy Spirit who gives us spiritual gifts), *and resurrection of the dead and eternal judgment* (at the second coming of Christ)".

This is the milk that newborn babes in Christ need to drink first (*Hebrews 5:13*). But because most believers remain babes all their lives, they never go on to experience the solid food of the full gospel.

Such were the Hebrew Christians, and the Corinthian Christians.

Paul writing to the Christians at Corinth said, "*I determined not to know anything among you except Jesus Christ and Him crucified*" (*1 Corinthians 2:2*).

Why couldn't he tell them anything beyond the fact that Christ had died for their sins and been raised from the dead (*1 Corinthians 15:1–4*)?

He explains the reason in *1 Corinthians 3:2*: Because they were *babes*, unable to digest solid food. They had not responded sufficiently even to the foundational truth that they had been taught. So Paul could not lead them further. And so they remained carnal, defeated by strife and jealousy, and party spirit, etc.

When people are babes, we cannot teach them anything beyond '*Jesus Christ and Him crucified*'. Thus, such believers remain carnal.

"*But,*" says Paul to the Corinthian 'babes', "*we do speak God's wisdom among those who are mature* (that is, among those in other churches, who could eat solid food) ... *the hidden wisdom which God predestined before the ages to our glory*" (*1 Corinthians 2:6, 7*).

The church in Ephesus was one such church where Paul could preach the full gospel.

What is the full gospel?
We can look at the Old Testament tabernacle and learn some lessons concerning it from there.

The tabernacle was a God-given symbol of His dwelling place. In its symbolism, we can see what the full gospel is and how we can enter into the enjoyment of God's presence and His full purpose for our lives.

The tabernacle had three parts to it – the outer court, the holy place and the most holy place – representing three parts of the full gospel.

The First Part of the Gospel – Jesus Our Saviour

In the outer court, there were the altar of sacrifice and the laver of water (for washing). The altar represents the message of '*Christ crucified for our sins*'. The laver represents the external cleansing of our lives (*Hebrews 10:22*), and the washing of regeneration (*Titus 3:5*) that we testify to in the baptism in water (*Acts 22:16*).

This is the first stage of the Christian life, where a person repents and trusts in Jesus as his Saviour – who bore the penalty for his sins – and is then baptized in water.

The Second Part of the Gospel – Jesus Our Baptizer

Whereas the outer court was open to all the Israelites (but not to the heathen), the Holy Place was open only to the priests – to those who were engaged in the service of the Lord.

In the Old Testament, the most important requirement to serve the Lord – whether as a prophet, priest or king – was the '*anointing of the Holy Spirit*'. No human qualification could be a substitute for this anointing. Even Jesus did not step out into His public ministry without first being anointed with the Holy Spirit. The Lord desires to lead His children from 'the outer court' into this realm – to the anointing of the Spirit and the exercise of spiritual gifts for His service.

The Holy Place had three items of furniture in it:

1. The lampstand – which symbolised the anointing giving us power to be witnesses for Christ (*Acts 1:8*).
2. The table of showbread – which symbolised the anointing giving us revelation on the Word (*2 Corinthians 3:18*).
3. The altar of incense – which symbolised the anointing giving us power in prayer (*Romans 8:26, 27*).

To reach thus far is to reach the second stage of Christian life – receiving not only the forgiveness of sins and water-baptism, but the baptism in the Holy Spirit as well.

The Third Part of the Gospel – Jesus Our Forerunner

The Most High Place, was where the glory of God dwelt in the tabernacle. Like the New Jerusalem (which symbolises the church), this too was an exact cube: "*Its length, width and height are equal*" (*Revelation 21:16*).

No person – not even a priest – was permitted to go into the Most Holy Place. Even the High Priest could go in only once a year to atone for the sins of the people. This highlighted the fact that the way into the immediate presence of God was still not open for any man (*Hebrews 9:8*).

We learn thereby that even the finest of Old Testament saints could go only as far as the Holy Place, in terms of their spiritual experience.

John the Baptist was the greatest person born of women up until the birth of Jesus. He was greater even than Mary, as Jesus said in *Matthew 11:11*. Yet Jesus went on to say that the least one who entered the kingdom of God would be greater than even John the Baptist. Why?

Old Testament saints could receive a number of blessings from God. They could receive forgiveness of sins (as David received – *Psalm 103:3*) and be justified by faith (as Abraham was – *Genesis 15:6; Romans 4:2, 3*). They could also come to an external righteousness of life (as Zacharias and Elisabeth came to – *Luke 1:6*) and be anointed for service (as Gideon and Elisha were – *Judges 6:34; 2 Kings 2:9–15*).

In other words, they could come into the Outer Court and even into the Holy Place. But when they came to the veil curtaining-off the Most Holy Place, they could not proceed any further. ***They could not partake of God's nature.***

Under the New Covenant however, the way has been opened for us to enter right through the veil into the Most Holy Place. We are told in *Hebrews 10:19, 20* that we now have *"confidence to enter the (most) holy place by the blood of Jesus, by a new and living way which He inaugurated for us through the veil, that is, His flesh"*.

The temple in Jerusalem (built according to the pattern of the tabernacle) also had a veil between the Holy Place and the Most Holy Place. This was torn from top to bottom, when Jesus died on Calvary (*Matthew 27:50, 51*). This signified a finished work that Jesus had done in His flesh.

The secret of living a godly life (we are told in *1 Timothy 3:16*) lies in knowing that Christ came in the flesh and kept His spirit pure and undefiled. It is thus that the way into the Most Holy Place has been opened for us to enter in.

Man's self-will is the thick *"veil"* that blocks off the presence of God from him. Jesus denied His own will at all times during His earthly life. It was thus that He kept His spirit pure. We too can walk the same way, if we *"crucify the flesh* (self-will) *with its passions and desires"* (*Galatians 5:24*). We can then dwell in the Most Holy Place always as Jesus did.

When the apostle writes to the Hebrews, contrasting milk with solid food (*Hebrews 5:13*), he tells them that the truth ('solid food') was *"difficult to explain"* (*verse 11*). That truth (as the context clearly shows in *Hebrews 5:7–10*) referred to Christ in the days of His flesh, praying with loud crying and tears, suffering, obeying and being made complete.

Just as it was difficult for many believers to receive this truth in the first century, it is difficult for most believers to receive it today also. And the reason is the same – because they are *"dull of hearing"* (*Hebrews 5:11*). And they are dull of hearing because they are content with their sub-standard defeated state.

But God gives revelation to those who are hungering and thirsting for a godly life. The secret of the Lord is whispered in the ears of those who fear Him (*Psalm 25:14*). Thus they find the secret of perfection.

In the Most Holy Place we can have the righteous requirement of God's Law fulfilled within us (*Romans 8:3, 4*). We can partake of the Divine nature. God is Love and the righteous requirement of the law can be summed up in one word: *LOVE* – that is, loving the Lord with all our hearts and loving our neighbours as ourselves.

"Godliness" or partaking of the Divine Nature of LOVE, was impossible for people under the Old Covenant, because the Holy Spirit could not dwell in people's hearts then. But that is now possible. This is the pearl of great value, to possess which, we must give up all other pearls.

God is Love and "the one who abides in love abides in God" (*1 John 4:16*). One who does not live in love cannot live in God's presence. The Bible says that "love is as strong as death" (*Song of Solomon 8:6*). That means that just as death spares no one but comes upon all human beings, even so God's love also comes upon all human beings. In the New Covenant, where death has been conquered by Jesus, we could say that "Divine love is stronger than death". The love of God manifested by Jesus could not be overcome by all the hatred and venom and bitterness (spiritual death) that was hurled at Jesus during His earthly life. The light of God's love shone in the darkness and the darkness could not overcome it.

It is only when our self-will is crucified through the power of the Holy Spirit that we can live in the Most Holy Place and love everyone with divine love.

With most believers (even with many who preach holiness) their love is restricted to those within *their own group*. They may never speak *evil* of anyone in their *own* group, but they feel quite free to *speak and hear evil* about *other* believers. Examine your-self, dear reader, and see if that is not true of your own life. Such 'love' is human love, not divine. When believers are satisfied with such an exclusive 'ghetto-mentality', they never rise any further.

Jesus came to make us both good and loving like the Father, who makes His sun to rise on all people – irrespective of their attitude towards Him.

Jesus was tempted in every point as we are (*Hebrews 4:15*). In other words, He was tempted to do His own will and please Himself in numerous ways. God took His Son, during the 33½ years that He was on earth, through the entire range of tempta-tions possible to man. And Jesus came through triumphant in every one of them. He never once yielded to His self-will. Thus He never sinned even once, in thought, word, deed, attitude or motive. Self-will becomes sin only when it is yielded to.

This was the "*education*" the Jesus went through during His earthly life: He learned obedience, when obedience meant suffer-ing (*Hebrews 5:8*). And the suffering referred to here is suffering that comes through denying one's own will.

The opposite of suffering is enjoyment. There are two options that we all have whenever we are tempted – either to *enjoy* the pleasure of doing what pleases us or to *suffer* by putting our self-will to death. Jesus chose to suffer consistently. "*He never pleased Himself*" (*Romans 15:3*).

By the time Jesus died on the cross, He had gone through the entire range of temptations possible for man and come out triumphant in every one of them. On the eve of His crucifixion, He could say, "*Father, I have finished the work You gave Me to do*" (*John 17:4*). And with the completion of His offering Himself on the cross, the veil was rent. The way into the Most Holy Place was open at last.

2 Corinthians 4:10 says that "*we always carry about in the body the dying of Jesus so that the life of Jesus also may be manifested in our body.*" What does the "*dying of Jesus*" mean here? We can have no part in the death that Jesus died on Calvary's cross, where He died for the sins of the world. There He died alone. There He rent the veil and opened the new and living way for us. We don't have to rend the veil a second time now, for it has already been rent. The way into God's presence is permanently open. But we have to walk the way of the rent veil – the way of the cross. We are to share in His perpetual "*dying*" – the dying to our self-will.

Jesus is our Forerunner who walked this way of self-denial before us. Through this new and living way that He inaugurated for us, we can dwell in the Most Holy Place all the days of our life. This is not a once-for-all experience like entering through a door. It is a way that we must walk on, day by day – taking up our cross daily.

You can live in the Most Holy Place one day and be back in the Holy Place or the Outer Court the next day, if you are not careful. You can even end up outside God's tabernacle, if you live according to the flesh (*See Romans 8:13*). It takes only 24 hours for a person to backslide and for his heart to be hardened. It takes only 24 hours to become bitter towards someone whom we had once forgiven. That is why we are told to exhort one another DAILY (within every 24-hour period), to avoid backsliding. If we don't have a brother or sister to exhort us daily, we must allow God's word and the Holy Spirit to exhort us DAILY (*Hebrews 3:13*).

> The full gospel then is that "*what the Law could not do, weak as it was through the flesh, God did*" (*Romans 8:3, 4*). In other words, what was not possible under the old covenant – namely, having victory over sin in our inner life, and partaking of God's nature – is now possible. God has made a way for us to partake of His own nature of LOVE.

When a person enters into the Most Holy Place, he enters the third stage of the Christian life – the highest stage.

In the Most Holy Place, only God dwells. Those who dwell here dwell with God and have been freed from people – freed from seeking the honour of men and even of Christian leaders. They have also been freed from being offended, from complaining and grumbling, and from bitterness and envy. They are now free to love others even as Jesus loved them, irrespective of whether they are loved in return or not.

They now seek the honour of God alone, in all that they do – being more conscious of God than of people, when they pray and speak in the meetings for example. They fear God and therefore their inner (hidden) life is as pure as their external life.

Those who dwell here have seen that all that is big and great in the eyes of men is an abomination in God's sight. They now consider everything as rubbish compared to the possibility of partaking of the nature of God in Christ.

Having entered into a life of victory over sin, they are kept from falling by the power of God and partake of the glory of God, more and more. They always give thanks for everything and they live before the face of God in all that they do.

Those who dwell in the Most Holy Place receive increasing discernment, in God's light, on what is only soulish (human) and what is really spiritual (divine).

There is a lot of difference between imitating Jesus and partaking of His nature. When we imitate Him, life is a constant struggle. But when we partake of His nature, we come to *rest*.

We all know how easy it was for us as children of Adam, to hate, tell lies, get angry, lust after women, seek man's honour, love money, and be selfish and proud – because that was our nature. When we partake of the divine nature, it can become just as easy for us to love, speak the truth, be patient, pure, generous, unselfish and humble and seek the glory of God.

It is easy for a cat to lick its body and keep itself clean at all times. That is not a strain for a cat, for that is its nature. But for a pig to do that – imitating the cat – would be a constant strain. That illustrates the difference between partaking of a nature and trying to imitate it.

God gives us His own life – *"the life of Jesus"* (*2 Corinthians 4:10*). Thus we can partake of God's goodness, which is His glory. Then it won't be a strain for us to be good to those who are evil to us, or to forgive those who sin against us. We can continue in this Divine goodness until the end of our lives, just like a cat continues to lick itself clean until the end of its life.

It is in the Most Holy Place also that people are formed together into a functioning Body (as opposed to a mere congregation). There is no individualism in the Most Holy Place. No one here lives unto himself. Everyone who lives here is a perpetual sacrifice and therefore God is able to make all such brothers and sisters into the functioning Body of Christ with spiritual authority in a locality. It is about those who live here that Jesus spoke as 'agreeing' and having authority to receiving anything they ask for from the Father, and who can bind Satan's power at will (*Matthew 18:18–20*).

In every assembly of Christians, the vast majority dwell in the Outer Court – having responded to one-third of the gospel message. Some progress into the Holy Place – being anointed by the Holy Spirit. These have responded to two-thirds of the gospel message. But the spiritual authority and effectiveness of that assembly (as far as God is concerned), is measured in terms of the number who have entered into the Most Holy Place (those who have responded to *the full gospel*).

Satan fears only those who have gone through the veil into the Most Holy Place. This is why he has blinded believers to the full gospel.

It is only when there is a central core in an assembly of those who dwell permanently in the Most Holy Place, that the assembly can be kept pure from the forces of spiritual death and preserved in the way of life.

The Bride of Christ becomes one flesh with her Bridegroom.

"The two shall become one flesh – this is a great mystery, but I am speaking with reference to Christ and the church" (Ephesians 5:31, 32).

Don't be satisfied then with anything less than God's highest for your life. Do violence to all sin that would stand in your way and also to all the traditions and opinions of man that would hinder you from pressing on into the place that Jesus has inaugurated and opened for you.

2

The Balance of Truth

*"If you leave God's paths and go astray (to the right or to the left),
you will hear a Voice behind you say, 'No, this is the way; walk here'"*
(Isaiah 30:20, 21 - TLB).

The Voice referred to here is the voice of the Holy Spirit Who alerts us when we go even slightly astray (to the right or to the left) from the straight and narrow path that leads to the throne of God.

When we look at even the churches of believers today, we find that most of them have got into a rut – either to the right or to the left of the straight line of truth.

Consider just one example: Some groups over-emphasise the gifts of the Spirit and are imbalanced in one direction. Others over-emphasise the fruit of the Spirit and neglect the gifts altogether and are thus imbalanced the other way. Neither of these groups seems to be listening to the Voice that is trying to tell them to move to the left/right in order to get back to the centre. Each group has its own favourite verses from the Bible that they keep going back to again and again. They never seem to see other portions of Scripture that could make them balanced, because they are prejudiced against those verses.

Very often their refusal to see those other verses is due to the fact that those other verses have been misused by the groups that have gone astray in the opposite direction. So their understanding of truth has come from a reaction to the extremes that other groups have gone to, and not from a careful study of all of God's Word.

The ministry of the prophets in the Old Testament was always to point out where Israel was going astray. They spoke forth the corrective word of the Holy Spirit. They did not seek for a "balanced ministry". They always stressed what was missing. They never wasted time speaking of the matters in Israel that were already according to God's order. In that sense the Old Testament prophets were all imbalanced in their ministry.

Consider Jeremiah, for example. At one stage, Jeremiah said to God, "You have NEVER ONCE let me speak a word of kindness to these people. Always it is disaster, horror and destruction" (*Jeremiah 20:8* - TLB). His was certainly not a balanced message full of grace and truth!! It was just judgment, judgment and more judgment! This message became such a burden to Jeremiah himself at one stage. But he still could not quit preaching it, because every time he thought of changing the message, God's Word of judgment would burn within his heart like a fire and he could not hold it in any longer (*Jeremiah 20:9* - TLB). And so he continued preaching judgment to the nation of Judah for 46 years.

If Jeremiah had listened to the voice of his own reason or to the advice of other preachers who did not know the mind of God, he would have modified his message. He would then have been more balanced. But he would not have been God's prophet any longer!

Now consider the ministry of an earlier prophet, Hosea. His message was totally different from Jeremiah's. God's message through Hosea to Israel was, "O how I love you, even though you have disobeyed me and gone astray." But Jeremiah, who lived 180 years after Hosea, never sought to imitate Hosea's ministry. These prophets were not imitators of each other. Each of them knew the burden that God had given them.

A new-covenant prophet too will always speak of what is lacking in a church, and point out where it is imbalanced. He will have discernment from God about the current need of the people to whom he ministers.

The greatest need in every church today is for prophetic ministry – through which the Spirit speaks saying, "No. Not that way. This way."

Most preachers prepare their sermons by reading books and magazines (like HIDDEN TREASURES) and by listening to tapes – in order to impress their hearers. They are careful however, to leave out whatever might offend their hearers, because they seek for honour and for gifts.

Prophets however, are not like that. They listen to God, and tell the people exactly what God wants them to hear. And so a prophet may preach on one theme repeatedly, until the imbalance in a church is corrected. Professional preachers however are afraid of preaching the same message even twice to the same congregation. Travelling preachers even have to make a note (in their minds or in their diaries) as to what message they preached in a particular church, so that they don't make the mistake of preaching the same message again when they visit that church a second time – lest they lose their honour as preachers!!

What a desperate need there is for prophets in our day!

A teaching ministry is different from a prophetic ministry. The teacher is able to explain the doctrines of Scripture clearly. His teaching need not however, be related to the current need among the people he is ministering to. A teaching ministry on justification, or on the baptism in the Holy Spirit, or on sanctification, or on the second coming of Christ will always be profitable in any church! But the people there may still be defeated by sin and discouragement in spite of all this wonderful teaching. What such a church needs then is a prophetic ministry!

Let us consider one area where we need to be balanced: In our understanding of the gospel message.

In Ephesians, we see clearly the good news that Paul preached. Paul said to the elders of the church in Ephesus, after spending three years in their midst, "I declared to you the WHOLE purpose of God" (*Acts 20:27*).

Paul received the gospel-message directly from the mouth of the Lord Himself – and not second-hand from the mouths of other men, as all of us have received it (*Galatians 1:11, 12*). He said that if anyone preached any other gospel than the one he had received from the Lord, such a man would be cursed of God (*Galatians 1:8, 9*). It is that serious to preach any other gospel – or to dilute the gospel in any way or to leave out any part of it.

The letter to the Ephesians is divided into two parts – the first three chapters form the first part of the gospel, and the next three chapters form the second part. The first part deals with what God has done for us. The second part deals with what we must do for God.

Ephesians 4:1 begins with, "Therefore, I entreat you to walk...". The word "Therefore..." indicates that all that follows in *chapters 4 to 6* is based on the foundation that the Holy Spirit has laid in the first three chapters. Paul was a good master-builder and he wrote Ephesians carefully, under the inspiration of the Holy Spirit.

Ephesians 4 to 6 we could say is the superstructure – built on the foundation of *Ephesians 1 to 3*. The imbalance that one sees in many groups in Christendom today is that some have built the foundation of the first 3 chapters, but have no superstructure on it. Others are building the superstructure (of the last 3 chapters), but without the foundation. Both groups are equally foolish.

Something to notice about the first three chapters in Ephesians is that there is not even one command or exhortation in all those chapters, as to what WE are to do in order to please God! On the other hand, they are full of a description of what GOD has done for us.

But notice that the next three chapters of Ephesians are full of exhortations as to how we are to please God!

That is a difference that must be carefully noted, if we are to distinguish between foundational truths and superstructural truths. We don't place doors and windows in the foundation! No! They are meant to be in the superstructure. But the superstructure itself must be built on the foundation. In other words, every commandment that we preach must be based firmly on what God has done FOR us and IN us in the first place.

If we are not sure first of all, of what God has done FOR us and IN us, then we will find ourselves incapable of keeping His commandments. We will then get into the same bondage that the old covenant saints got into, when they tried to keep God's laws and failed constantly. This is why many Christians too live a life of constant failure and discouragement, and feel that a life of victory is impossible for them.

It is true that a life of constant victory is impossible, if we do not have the foundation of *Ephesians 1 to 3* underneath us at all times. The foundation is not something that we lay once somewhere, and then go on and build the building itself somewhere itself.

Every building is not only built on its foundation, it continues to remain on the same foundation at all times. If new floors are added later on to the building, those floors too are built to rest on the same foundation that was initially laid for the building.

It is when believers lay a foundation in one place and then begin to build the superstructure somewhere else, that the Voice of the Holy Spirit will say to them (if they have ears to hear, and are not prejudiced), "No, not there. Build over here, where the foundation has been laid".

On the other hand, to those who have laid the foundation, and then do nothing else but admire the foundation (at every Sunday meeting!!), the Voice of the Holy Spirit will say (again if they have ears to hear, and are not prejudiced),

> "What are you going to do now? Are you happy with just the foundation? Don't you want to build the house?"

For those of us who have heard nothing but exhortation after exhortation from the pulpit for many years (based on the commands in *Ephesians 4 to 6*), what we now need to hear is a little more of the truth found in *Ephesians 1 to 3*, so as to be balanced.

Those who rush past *Ephesians 1 to 3*, will find later on in their lives, that they face the problems of insecurity, depression, fear, uncertainty of God's acceptance, jealousy, a competitive spirit, and many other evils.

Let us ask ourselves three questions and thereby have a check-up:

1. Have we ever felt when faced with a particular problem one day, that God would not help us with that problem, because we did not take time to pray or to read the Bible that particular morning?
2. Have we ever felt when we had an accident or when we faced some financial loss, that that happened because we did not spend time alone with God that morning?
3. Have we ever felt that because we did have a good lengthy time of Bible-reading and prayer one morning, that God had accepted us a little more that day than He did on other days?

If any of the above are true in your case, it would indicate that you have not yet been properly founded on *Ephesians 1 to 3*. You have not yet understood the basis on which God accepts you.

It is impossible to lead an overcoming life, if we are not firmly and securely founded on the fact of God's accepting us in Christ, on the basis of what Christ has done for us – and not on the basis of what we have done.

It is equally impossible to be an overcomer, if we only have the foundation, and never pay heed to the commandments and exhortations found in the New Testament.

We should not make either mistake.

The Foundation in *Ephesians 1 to 3*

"Blessed be the God and Father of our Lord Jesus Christ, WHO HAS BLESSED US with every spiritual blessing (every blessing of the Holy Spirit) *in the heavenly places in Christ"* (Ephesians 1:3).

The Bible begins with the words, "In the beginning God..." (*Genesis 1:1*).

That is how the true gospel begins too – with God and what He has done for us. A humanistic gospel however would begin with, "In the beginning man...". It would begin with what WE have to do, and not with what GOD has already done for us.

In fact this is one way to distinguish the true gospel from every false one. All cults proclaim a humanistic gospel that exalts human effort, where men can glory in what they have achieved.

Many such false gospels sound very good and appear to lead people towards holiness, and therefore many sincere believers are deceived. But all such gospels and those who proclaim them come under the curse that Paul proclaimed in *Galatians 1*.

Remember that the true gospel always begins with God, and with what He has done for us – and not with what man has to do for God.

So Ephesians begins with, "Blessed be GOD WHO HAS BLESSED US...". That is the right way to begin.

With how many blessings of the Holy Spirit has God blessed you?

Every single one of them. Not even one blessing has been left out.

You are an heir to EVERY single blessing of the Holy Spirit, the moment you are born again. It may take time before you appropriate all of those blessings to yourself. But don't forget that you are an heir to all of them from the very beginning.

"He chose us in Christ before the foundation of the world" (*Ephesians 1:4*).

Long before the universe was created, God knew each of us by name. Did you know that God knew you by name, millions of years ago? This assurance by itself can bring tremendous security into our lives.

"...that the eyes of your heart may be enlightened that you may know what are the riches of the glory of His inheritance in the saints." (Ephesians 1:18)

We must be rooted in this assurance that God got a treasure when He got you and me. That is the meaning of the above verse. *Zephaniah 3:17* states that God rejoices over us with shouts of joy.

Most believers live with the understanding that God is always looking at them with a frown and with an attitude that seems to say, "That's not good enough. You can do better". They can never imagine God rejoicing over them with shouts of joy! Yet that is what the Bible says clearly that God does.

"...that the eyes of your heart may be enlightened that you may know what is the surpassing greatness of His power toward us who believe...which He wrought in Christ when He raised Him from the dead" (*Ephesians 1:18–20*).

The greatest manifestation of God's power was not in creation, but in the resurrection of Christ.

This resurrection-power (greater than the power that created an universe from nothing) is what is now available to all of us who believe.

Everything is dependent on faith – and faith comes from hearing God speaking to us through His Word. So it is important to meditate on passages like the one above – and not rush through them.

Either what we read in *verses 18 to 20* (above) is a total lie or it is absolutely true. If it is a lie, then everything else that the New Testament teaches about forgiveness and justification etc., must also be false. On the other hand if we have seen that those other teachings were true, when we believed, then the reason why we don't experience this supernatural power of God in our lives, is because we do not believe!.

This power is available to all "who BELIEVE".

Jesus taught us to begin our prayers by saying, "Our Father Who art in heaven". We must be clear in our minds first of all, that we are talking, not to the Managing Director of the universe, but to our Father – a Father Who loves us, Who is intensely interested in every aspect of our lives, and Who is perfectly wise and almighty in power.

It is easy to rush past this part of addressing God as Father thinking it is unimportant. But the way we address God is the foundation for all prayer – faith in a loving Father Who knows our every need.

Jesus sought to lead his disciples to a firm faith in God as their Father. The first three chapters of Ephesians also seek to lead us to that same faith. Only such faith can bring perfect security into our lives. Otherwise our lives will be like a storm-tossed vessel – tossed by the winds and the waves of circumstances and the attacks of demonic forces.

Many believers are so insecure – perpetually unsure as to whether God will carry them but halfway across their earthly journey, and then cast them away, saying, "I have had enough of you". And so they are always trying to do something or the other to please God – giving a little extra money for Christian work perhaps, or fasting and praying etc., – in order to find acceptance with their Father.

An illustration will perhaps describe this condition more clearly.

Suppose you had three children of your own (aged between 10 and 6) and then you adopted a 8 year old boy from an orphanage. Your three children will feel perfectly free in your home and will sleep soundly at night and will be perfectly secure in your love at all times. But this boy who has come newly into your home, will always feel insecure. He will always wonder whether he is accepted in the same way as the others. He won't sleep soundly at night. No matter how much you reassure him, he will still have doubts about his being accepted as an equal with your other three children. One day when he spills his milk accidentally, he may wonder whether he will be thrown out of the house for that. He will feel that his acceptance with you will be dependent on his conduct. And so he will spend all his life trying to gain your acceptance.

This is a picture of the condition of most believers, in their attitude towards God. They are constantly striving to be accepted – and never seem to be sure that THEY HAVE ALREADY BEEN ACCEPTED IN CHRIST!

Ephesians 1 goes on to tell us that when God raised Christ from the dead, He put all things under His feet – and since Christ has been given to us as the Head of the church, all things are under our feet too! (*Ephesians 1:21, 22*).

That is why we can live in this world without any fear – either of men or of Satan. There is no demon anywhere in the universe that was not conquered by Jesus on the cross at Calvary.

When encountering demon-possessed people, I have conquered my own temptations to doubt and fear by asking myself this simple question, "Was this demon conquered by Jesus on Calvary or not?"

The answer to that is "Yes, he has been conquered" – every single time, without exception. Then I know that I have authority over that demon in Jesus' Name.

This has nothing to do with our abilities or gifts. It has only to do with what Christ did on Calvary, and with the fact that Christ is now our Head. Satan cannot touch us, when we are under Christ's headship.

Ephesians chapters 2 and 3 amplify further what has been mentioned in chapter 1. We can look briefly at some verses there. But you can meditate on the chapters themselves leisurely.

In *Ephesians 2:1–8*, we are told that when we were dead in our sins, God raised us up together with Christ and saved us.

A dead man can do absolutely nothing. So that means that when we could do absolutely nothing for ourselves, God raised us up and saved us. Do you believe that? Or do you feel that you did a little bit yourself too in order to help God to raise you from the dead?? That may sound funny. But there are multitudes of believers who feel that they did help God a little bit with their salvation!! It is obvious that such believers do not feel that they were dead in sin, but only perhaps sick with sin. A sick man may be able to do something. But a dead man can do nothing!!

What were you – sick or dead?

Read *Ephesians 2* carefully, and you will get the answer. You were dead – absolutely lifeless and dead! That is when God raised you up.

Our salvation was:

"not of ourselves"
"not of our works"
"that no-one should boast" (verse 8).

If our salvation was even a little bit because of our own works, we would have something to boast of. But because it was all of God, we give Him ALL the glory. And so none of us can boast over each other either. All who are proud have not understood the teaching of *Ephesians 2*.

Do you know that there is not a single verse in the Bible that says that Christ raised Himself from the dead? Everywhere it says that it was God Who raised Him. It was God Who raised us too.

Even if we were to live a blameless life on earth, one in which we pressed on to perfection for many years, yet at the end of it, when we stand before the Lord, we will still only be able to say, "Lord, I am a sinner deserving eternal hell. But You died for me. So I am saved by Your free grace. I have nothing at all to boast of."

Only one who realises this fact has understood the doctrine of salvation properly.

In *Ephesians 1:17, 18*, Paul had prayed that the Christians at Ephesus might receive revelation from the Holy Spirit.

At the end of this first half of Ephesians, in *chapter 3:16*, Paul prays that they might receive power from the Holy Spirit.

These are our two greatest needs – revelation and power.

The Holy Spirit alone can give us both.

The entire Christian life is dependent on the Holy Spirit. First of all the Spirit gives us revelation on what God has done for us in Christ.

Then He gives us power to walk in a manner worthy of our calling, obeying all that the Lord has taught us.

Let us now look at one last thing from *Ephesians 3*. In *verses 18 and 19* we see that we can experience the breadth and length and height and depth of the love of Christ (there are four dimensions there and that itself goes beyond human knowledge!!) – only along with ALL the saints.

We can never grasp the love of Christ all by ourselves. We need the other members of Christ's Body. And further, we need ALL the members of Christ's Body, not just those in our own little group.

That is why our hearts should always be open to ALL believers, even to those who don't agree with us, and even to those whom we would consider a bit extreme. We may not be able to work with all of them and we certainly will not be able to meet all of them on this earth. But our hearts should be open to all of God's children. Our hearts must have room for as many brothers and sisters, as God has children – both barbarian and cultured.

That is why we need to be open to read the writings of ALL godly people – and not just to the writings of our favourite authors.

Let me warn you in advance, that in my lifetime, I have found very, very few believers who have such an open heart. But those are the few who are truly spiritually wealthy. The remainder carry on with their poverty-stricken, sectarian attitudes and live and die as Pharisees, missing out on the wealth that could have been theirs, if they had been humble enough to accept all whom God had accepted.

Let us meditate carefully then on the first three chapters of Ephesians, and ask the Holy Spirit to give us revelation on these glorious truths that we have just been considering.

Once you have got revelation, you will be ready to seek the Spirit for His power to live an overcoming life, full of purity, humility and love.

Then we will be able to put away ALL unwholesome words from our speech, and ALL anger and ALL bitterness from our hearts (*Ephesians 4:29, 31*).

Then wives will be able to submit to their husbands as the church is to Christ, and husbands will be able to love their wives as Christ loved the church (*Ephesians 5:22, 25*).

Then we will be able to overcome Satan at all times (*Ephesians 6:11–13*).

And then we will have the power to "become imitators of God" (*Ephesians 5:1*).

God is able to do far more in us and through us than we can ask or think. To Him alone be all the glory (*Ephesians 3:20, 21*).

3

Having a Firm Grip on the Christian Life

God has given us five fingers on each hand. With these, we can hold on to things firmly. You could hold a glass with two fingers, but the grip won't be as firm as when you hold it with all five fingers.

In the same way, God has given us five gifts through which we can have firm grip on the Christian life. Where backsliding occurs, it is because believers relax their grip on one or more of these five areas.

As we begin a new year, let us determine that we shall not backslide any more, but progress – to know God, to walk in fellowship with Him and with our fellow-believers, and to be more available to Him for His service in the coming year, than we have ever been before.

1. The Blood of Christ

Forgiveness of our past sins is our very first and our constant need. The guilt of our sins could not be removed by God by any other way than by the payment of the full penalty for our sins. "Without the shedding of blood, there is no forgiveness" (*Hebrews 9:22*).

> When Christ shed His blood on the cross of Calvary, it purchased the pardon of every sin ever committed by anyone. But that pardon becomes ours only when we receive it. Through Christ's blood we now have the forgiveness of all our sins, if we sincerely turn from our sins (repent), trust in Him, and receive the forgiveness that he offers.

The blood of Christ also justifies us (*Romans 5:9*). This is more than just being forgiven. It is being declared righteous, just as though we had never sinned in our entire lives. God's promise is that "He will not remember our sins any more" (*Hebrews 8:12*). That means that He looks at us just as if we had never sinned.

That is the meaning of being justified. Such is the power of Christ's blood. Many believers live in perpetual condemnation concerning their past lives, because Satan has hid from them the fact that God has justified them through Christ's blood.

Through the blood of Christ we are redeemed (*1 Peter 1:18*). That means that we have been purchased from the slave-market of sin. The blood that Christ shed on Calvary was the ransom price that He paid to meet the demands of God's holy Law, so that we might be free, and not slaves any longer. We are born to be free. We need not be slaves any longer to Satan or men or to condemnation or guilt or fear or sin.

Through the blood of Christ, we are also brought into God's presence (*Ephesians 2:13*). God dwells in light that no man can approach. The only way to come into His presence is through the blood – till the end of our lives. However saintly we may become, our access to God's presence will always be through the blood of Christ. Many believers tend to forget this, once they get victory over conscious sin, and end up as Pharisees.

Through the blood shed on Calvary's cross, Christ has made peace with God (*Colossians 1:20*). God is not an Enemy to us now. This is a fact that needs to be established in our minds firmly. Many believers live with the feeling that God is constantly unhappy with them and is always frowning at them. This is Satan's lie, designed to bring believers into condemnation and to hinder their spiritual growth. Through the blood of Christ, we have become friends of God. Unless we believe this, we will never make any spiritual progress.

> The blood of Christ also cleanses us continually from all sin, when we walk in the light (*1 John 1:7*). To walk in the light is to walk in victory over all conscious sin. But even when we live in victory over conscious sin, there is still plenty of unconscious sin in all of us. That is why John goes on to say, "If we say we have no sin, we deceive ourselves" (*verse 8*).

It is not because we have a flesh, that we sin unconsciously, but because we have lived in conscious selfishness for many years, both prior to, and subsequent to our conversion. Jesus had the same flesh as we have. But because He never lived in selfishness at any time, He never sinned unconsciously even once. There was no sin at all in Him (*1 John 3:5*).

Our unconscious sins (which constitute perhaps about 90% of our total sins initially) are continually cleansed by Christ's blood, so that we can have constant, and unbroken fellowship with the Father.

Through the blood of Christ, we also overcome Satan and his accusations (*Revelation 12:11*). Satan accuses us to God, to other men and to ourselves constantly. But we can overcome his accusations by confessing ("the word of our testimony") that we have been forgiven, justified, redeemed, brought near to God, brought to peace with God and cleansed by the blood of Christ. Satan can have no power over us any longer.

We need the blood of Christ to cleanse us DAILY, for all of us sin unconsciously daily, and many believers sin consciously too.

2. The Holy Spirit

It is impossible to live a victorious Christian life or to serve God effectively, if we are not filled with the Holy Spirit.

Forgiveness of sins and the Holy Spirit are the two gifts that God offers to all repentant sinners AS SOON AS they turn to Him.

There is no need for anyone who turns to the Lord and receives forgiveness of sins to wait for even a single day before he receives the Holy Spirit. That is how it was in the early days of Christianity. In those days, as soon as people repented and believed, they were baptized in water and then received the Holy Spirit at once. That was part of their initial experience. But nowadays, we find believers waiting for years before being baptized in water and then waiting for many more years before receiving the Holy Spirit.

What every believer needs to know is that there is no need for any extra qualification in order to receive the Holy Spirit, other than what is required for the forgiveness of sins – namely, repentance from sin and faith in the Lord Jesus Christ. It is due to ignorance of this fact that many, many believers are not baptized in the Holy Spirit. If only they knew the truth, they would not be deceived by Satan any longer.

To try to be worthy enough to receive the Holy Spirit is as foolish as trying to be worthy enough to receive the forgiveness of sins.

The fullness of the Holy Spirit will primarily bring the fullness of the fruit of the Spirit in our lives – fullness of love, joy, peace, patience, kindness, goodness, faithfulness, gentleness, self-control (*Galatians 5:23*).

Secondly, it will equip us to be powerful witnesses for Christ and effective members of His earthly Body.

The anointing of the Holy Spirit is the prime requisite for being an effective member of Christ's Body. Without this, however holy our lives may be, we will be limited in our usefulness to God for His work on earth.

Although Jesus lived a pure and holy life for 30 years, He still needed to be anointed with the Holy Spirit, before He could have the supernatural gifts necessary for Him to fulfil His ministry.

God wants to equip us in the same way today, so that we can carry on that ministry, as the Body of Christ on earth. Those who either despise or don't believe in these supernatural gifts will of course not have them. Thus their service for the Lord will also be limited.

We need to be filled with the Holy Spirit DAILY, for this is not a once-for-all experience that takes care of our need forever.

3. The Word of God

Right from the first paragraph of Scripture, we see the Holy Spirit operating along with God's Word. The spoken Word of God and the brooding of the Holy Spirit (*Genesis 1:3*), brought beauty and order out of chaos. That is how God can bring beauty and order into our lives too.

The power of the Holy Spirit known experientially, without the guidance of the written Word would leave a man like a steam engine, full of steam but without any rails to run on. Conversely, knowledge of the written Word without the anointing and the power of the Holy Spirit would make a man like an engine standing on neatly laid-out rails, but lacking the steam to move forward.

God's Word is the means by which we understand the mind of God. Through submitting to it, we can have our minds renewed to think the way God thinks and "to look at things from God's point of view" (*Colossians 1:9* - paraphrase). It is impossible to grow spiritually without allowing God's Word to renew our minds. Many do not know the will of God in the different situations of life, only because they do not know the Word of God.

There is an answer in God's Word for every single problem that we can ever face in life – if only we know where to find it.

How poor those believers are who do not know the Word of God.

The Word of God is also a revealer of our inner spiritual condition (*Hebrews 4:12*). It is like an scanning machine that reveals everything inside our hearts. One who does not regularly meditate on God's Word will remain perpetually ignorant and self-deceived about his true state.

When it comes to spiritual battle, the Word of God is our weapon against Satan. Jesus overcame Satan only by quoting the Word of God to him (*Matthew 4:1–10*). This is the sword by which the Enemy is driven away. When the Word of God dwells within a person, he becomes strong to overcome all of Satan's schemes (*1 John 2:14*).

We need to hear God's Word speaking to us DAILY, if we are to get light on ourselves, be overcomers, and make spiritual progress.

4. The Way of the Cross

Jesus, as our Forerunner (One Who has run the same race ahead of us), has opened a way for us to enter the Father's presence and dwell there all the time. This way is called "the new and living way" (*Hebrews 10:20*).

Paul speaks of it as "always carrying about in the body the dying of Jesus" (*2 Corinthians 4:10*). He once said, as his personal testimony, that he was crucified with Christ and lived himself no longer. It was Christ that now lived in him, because he himself had died on Calvary. This was the secret of his amazing life and usefulness to God.

Jesus always walked the way of the cross – the way of death to Self. He NEVER pleased Himself even once (*Romans 15:4*). To please oneself is the essence of all sin. To deny oneself is the essence of holiness.

Jesus once said that no-one would be able to follow Him, unless he decided to deny himself DAILY and to die to himself DAILY (*Luke 9:23*). That is clear. It is impossible to follow Jesus if we don't deny ourselves daily. We may be cleansed in Christ's blood, have received the Holy Spirit and have a deep knowledge of the

Word. But if we don't die to ourselves daily, we cannot follow the Lord Jesus. That is certain.

Jesus once spoke of those who seek to patch up an old garment with a new patch. This He said would tear the garment. What was needed was to get rid of the old garment and get a brand new one. In another parable, He spoke of making the tree itself good, if we wanted the fruit to be good. It was no use just cutting off the bad fruit.

All these parables have basically one lesson: The old man cannot be improved. He has been crucified by God (*Romans 6:6*). Now we must agree with God's judgment on him, and put him off, and put on the new man.

> The way of the cross is the way of spiritual progress. If you are not overcoming sins like anger, irritation, impatience, lustful thinking, dishonesty, jealousy, malice, bitterness, and the love of money etc., the answer lies here: You have avoided the way of the cross.

A dead man does not stand up for his rights. He does not fight back. He does not care about his reputation. He will not take revenge. He cannot hate anyone or have a bitterness against anyone.

This is what it means to die to Self.

This way of the cross, like all the other provisions that God has made for our spiritual growth (that we considered above), is also something that we need DAILY, if we are to make spiritual progress.

5. The Body of Christ

Under the new covenant, God has not intended that we should be lone Christians living by ourselves – even if we are living in victory over sin. God's will is that there should be a Body of disciples of Jesus manifesting His glory together.

There is a difference between a Body and a congregation. A congregation is no better than a secular club. The club may be a good club, where people care for one another and help one another. But a Body is more than that. In the Body of Christ, each member is first of all inwardly connected to the Head and then inwardly and inseparably connected to the other members. These members must grow in oneness until their unity is like the unity of the Father and the Son (*John 17:21–23*).

Satan opposes the building of such a Body anywhere on earth, for he knows that such a Body can rout him, put him to flight, and destroy his kingdom. Jesus said that it is against the church that the gates of Hell would not prevail (*Matthew 16:18*). The gates of Hell may prevail against a lone individual Christian. But they cannot prevail against the church. That is why Satan's attacks on spiritual unity among believers are far stronger than his attacks on purity.

Where any two disciples of Jesus are firmly united in oneness of mind and spirit, whatever they ask for will be granted, for in two such disciples is found an expression of the Body of Christ (*Matthew 18:18–20*).

In fellowship with other believers, we will discover the selfishness and utter corruption of our flesh much more quickly and more deeply than if we lived all by ourselves. It is only through fellowship with others who have a flesh that our rough edges can be smoothened out.

Many believers merely spin theories about the church and the Body of Christ. But we must be among those who seek reality. There are enough theories about the church in Christendom. We don't have to add to that number with one more theory or doctrine about the Body of Christ. Let us demonstrate the reality of the Body in our mutual relationships in our local church, and thus demonstrate to the world and to Satan that the Body of Christ is a reality on earth.

Receiving All of God's Gifts

We can do many things with one finger, more with two fingers, still more with three fingers, and very much more with four fingers. But God in His wisdom has created us with five fingers, with a purpose. When we think of the fingers on our hands, we would never be satisfied with the bare minimum of two fingers.

Why then should we be satisfied with the bare minimum in the Christian life? Let us avail of ALL the gifts that God has given us to have a strong grip on the Christian life.

4

The Threefold Exchange at the Cross

Everything that God does for us is by grace through faith (*Ephesians 2:8*). Grace is God's hand reaching down from heaven offering us every spiritual blessing in heavenly places in Christ (*Ephesians 1:3*). Faith is our hand reaching up and taking those blessings from God's hand.

There are at least four reasons why believers remain defeated and poor when God would have them be overcomers and spiritually rich:

1. They are ignorant of the blessings God has given them in Christ.
2. Although they know about them, they do not ask God for them.
3. Although they ask for them, they ask in unbelief.
4. Although they ask in faith, they ask with selfish motives. (*John 8:32; Romans 10:14; James 4:2; John 16:24; Matthew 13:58; James 1:7; 4:3*).

The Bible begins with the words, "In the beginning God..." (*Genesis 1:1*). This is the primary characteristic of any work that is truly Divine: It has its origin in God Himself. On the other hand, human work – even if it is called "Christian work" – has its origin in the mind of man.

Jesus said, "Every plant which My heavenly Father did not plant will be rooted up." (*Matthew 15:13*). The plant (idea, work, ministry etc.,) itself may be a good plant. But that makes no difference. If it was not planted by God, it will be pulled out and burnt up one day.

There are many good things in Christendom today that did not originate in God. But in the day when God shakes heaven and earth, all of that will be destroyed by God Himself. Only that which is unshakable – that which originated in God – will remain in that day (*Hebrews 12:26–28*).

There is a strong urge in the flesh of man to want to do things for God. All false religions flourish by catering to this urge.

It makes man feel big and important when he feels that he has done something for God – whether it be building a temple or a mosque, or giving money to the poor, or practising righteousness, or preaching, or doing good.

In true Christianity however, everything begins with God.

"In Christ"

Our salvation began in God's mind. It was He Who "chose us in Christ before the foundation of the world" (*Ephesians 1:4*). We love Him because He first loved us (*1 John 4:19*). In Ephesians, Paul describes first of all what God has done for us (*Chapters 1 to 3*). Only then does he proceed to describe what we must do for God (*Chapters 4 to 6*).

In evangelical circles, the phrase "accepting Christ" is very commonly used. Although the New Testament does speak about "Christ IN us" (*Colossians 1:27*; *Ephesians 3:17*), it speaks much more about OUR BEING IN CHRIST.

Accepting Christ is what WE do, whereas placing us in Christ is what GOD does. It is not surprising therefore that a man-centred theology places much more emphasis on what we do rather than on what God does. If we want our Christian life to be strong, we must first of all be rooted and grounded in what God has done for us IN CHRIST.

To illustrate what it means to be "in Christ", consider a piece of paper placed inside a book. If the book is posted to Bombay, the paper also goes to Bombay. Similarly, since we were placed in Christ before the foundation of the world, when Christ was crucified on Calvary's hill, we were crucified in Him too. When He was buried, we were buried in Him. And when He was raised, we were raised in Him. When He ascended, we ascended in Him. And where He is now, we are – IN HIM.

Only if we believe this truth of God's Word, can we experience it – not otherwise. "According to your faith be it unto you", is a law of God.

It is something like God having put millions of rupees in our bank account and then giving us blank cheque-leaves signed with Jesus' Name on them (*2 Corinthians 1:20*). All we have to do now is fill in the amount and go to the bank and claim our inheritance – in Jesus' Name.

The good news of the gospel centres primarily around what God has done for us in our Lord Jesus Christ. Because of what Christ has done for us, we can have a foretaste of heaven in our hearts right now.

Heaven is a place of perfect peace and perfect joy. No-one is ever gloomy or depressed or sour or bitter in heaven. No-one is fearful in heaven, because there is no problem that God cannot solve. The gospel message is that we can enter into that heavenly life now itself.

Why is heaven such a wonderful place? Basically because no-one does his own will in heaven. Everyone does the will of God. This is why Jesus taught us to pray: "Our Father Who art in heaven. Thy will be done on earth as it is in heaven". When that is our sincere prayer, the atmosphere of heaven will pervade every part of our hearts too.

Those who pray that prayer will eagerly seek to find God's will – as a husband or a wife, as a father or a mother, or as a brother or a sister in the church. And they will want to do God's will in its entirety. To such believers, the will of God will not be a burden, but a joy and a delight. They will never be depressed or gloomy or fearful, for they know that they can never face a problem that God cannot solve.

> When Jesus said, "I have come down from heaven, not to do My own will, but the will of Him Who sent Me" (*John 6:38*), He was saying that He had come to earth to bring the atmosphere of heaven to earth. And throughout His life on earth, He demonstrated what it was to live with the atmosphere of heaven ruling His life. Wherever Jesus went He was a blessing to others. This is the life that He now wants to give us too.

But in order to enter into this life, we must first understand what God did for us in Christ on the cross.

Our life is like a building. The foundation is what God does for us, and the superstructure is what we do for God. No building can be strong without a strong foundation. Herein lies the reason for failure in the lives of many Christians: Without being gripped first with what God has done for them in Christ, they have stepped out seeking to do things for God. The end result is always depression and frustration.

The Bible teaches that Jesus took our place on the cross. He exchanged places with us. There are three areas where this exchange took place. When we accept this exchange in faith, we can become what God wants us to become in these three areas:

1. Jesus Became Sin in Order to Make Us Righteous

"God made Christ Who knew no sin to be sin on our behalf, that we might become the righteousness of God in Him" (2 Corinthians 5:21).

Christ became sin for us so that we might become the righteousness of God IN HIM. This is justification, and it is a free gift of God for those who are humble enough to recognize that they can never become righteous enough to meet God's holy standards. It is by grace alone that we are justified, and as the Bible says, "If it is by grace, it is no longer on the basis of works, otherwise grace is no longer grace" (*Romans 11:6*).

Those who seek to become righteous before God on the basis of their good works (putting the flesh to death etc.,) will fail just like Israel failed (Read *Romans 9:31, 32* and *10:3* carefully). Only those who seek to be justified by faith will attain to God's righteousness (*Romans 9:30*).

Many believers in their eagerness to get victory over sin, take a long jump from *Romans 3:23* ("All have sinned and fall short of the glory of God") to *Romans 6:14* ("Sin shall not be master over you"), bypassing the process of justification by faith described in *Romans 3:24 to 5:21*. As a result they become Pharisees. Two clear evidences of their Pharisaism are their pride in their own "holiness", and their despising of others who they feel are not as "holy" as they are!!

Jesus not only bore the punishment for our sins. He actually BECAME SIN. We cannot fully understand how awful an experience that was for our Lord, because we have unfortunately become as familiar with sin as a pig is with eating human dung. To understand, even faintly, the revulsion that Jesus had for sin, consider two illustrations:

Think first of what it means to jump into a septic tank that is full of human dung, and to become assimilated with it permanently. Or think of what it means to voluntarily receive a dreadful, incurable disease that covers your whole body with sores from head to feet.

Even those illustrations are imperfect and can give us only a faint picture of the depth of Christ's love for us, that made Him choose voluntarily to become what He hated, in order that we might become the righteousness of God in Him. Only when we see Jesus face to face will we be able to understand fully what it cost Him to save us. But even now we should be able to see something of the awfulness of sin and learn to hate it – when we see that it was our sin that crucified Christ.

Basically, there are two grounds on which Satan constantly seeks to accuse us: (1) Our past sins; and (2) Our present state. Thus he robs us of our confidence before God. But God has made provision in the gospel for a solution to both these problems.

> To solve the problem of our past sins, God "justifies us through Christ's blood" (*Romans 5:9*). The blood of Christ cleanses us so thoroughly from our past record, that God promises not even to remember our past sins (*Hebrews 8:12*). If God remembers none of our past sins, then we can truthfully say that He looks at us just as if we had never sinned in our entire life!! The Devil will try his best to prevent you from believing this truth. If you believe Satan's lie, you will live in condemnation perpetually, and never be bold to come before God. But if you resist Satan, "through the blood of the Lamb, and the word of your testimony" concerning your being cleansed in Jesus' blood, you can be an overcomer (*Revelation 12:11*).
>
> To solve the problem of our present state, God places us in Christ. Nothing good dwells in our flesh. Even if we put the flesh to death for a hundred years, we will still be unfit to stand before God. This was why God forbade the Israelites from entering within the veil into the Most Holy Place of the tabernacle, where He dwelt. That veil symbolised the flesh which prevented man from coming before God's face (*Hebrews 10:20*).

God's righteousness is as high above the righteousness of the holiest man on earth, as heaven is above the earth (*Isaiah 55:8, 9*). Even sinless angels cannot look at God's face, but have to cover their faces before Him (*Isaiah 6:2, 3*). Only Christ can look straight into the Father's face. And so God places us in Christ, so that we can now come before Him, without any fear – because we are in Christ. God justifies us by placing us in Christ, and accepting us as being as righteous as Christ Himself.

We can rejoice now in our perfect acceptance before God, because we have become the righteousness of God in Christ. The preaching of "any other gospel" that teaches acceptance before God on the basis of the works of the Law will bring the curse of God upon such a preacher (*Galatians 1:8*). Only after perfectly justifying us, does God lead us on to sanctification – a life of victory over sin and partaking of His nature.

2. Jesus Became Poor in Order to Make Us Rich

"Though the Lord Jesus Christ was rich, yet for your sake He became poor, that you through His poverty might become rich" (2 Corinthians 8:9).

Christ became poor for us, that we might become rich IN HIM.

The poverty and wealth spoken of in this verse could be taken spiritually. But the context in which the verse appears indicates that the Holy Spirit is speaking of material poverty and material riches as well.

What does it mean "to be rich"? It does not mean having plenty of money and property, but rather having enough to meet our needs and some extra to help and bless others with.

Being rich is described in *Revelation 3:17* as "having need of nothing". That is how God is rich. God does not have silver or gold or a bank account or even a wallet. But He has need of nothing.

Jesus was not poor when He was on earth, for He had "need of nothing". He could even provide a meal once for about 10,000 people – 5000 men, and a number of women and children (*Matthew 14:21*). Only a rich man could do that! He had enough money to pay His taxes (*Matthew 17:27*). He never had to borrow money from anyone at any time. And He even had enough money to give to the poor (*John 13:29*).

Jesus once said, "The poor you have with you always, but you do not always have Me" (*Matthew 26:11*). There He contrasted Himself with the poor. On another occasion, when Jesus told a rich young ruler to give all his money to the poor, Jesus was certainly not including Himself also among the poor to whom the money was to be given!! No. It is clear that Jesus was rich when He was on earth in this sense: He lacked nothing.

The early apostles too were not poor. When they told the believers "to remember the poor" (*Galatians 2:10*), they were not asking the believers to remember them!! No. Those apostles may not have had silver and gold (*Acts 3:6*). But they had all that they needed. In this way they were rich like their Master before them. That is how God wants us to be rich too.

But we see that Jesus did become poor when he hung on the cross. A poor man is described in the New Testament as one who has "threadbare clothing" (*James 2:2*). The poorest beggar we have seen in India usually has at least a torn rag around his body. But Jesus did not have even that when He was crucified. He was stripped naked and crucified. He really became poor for our sakes, when He was crucified.

Jesus became poor on the cross, so that we might become rich – or in other words, that we might have "need of nothing" in our lives. God has not promised to give us all that we want, but all that we need (*Philippians 4:19*). Wise parents do not give their children all that they want or ask for, but only all that they need. So with God too.

The old covenant promised earthly wealth to those who obeyed the Law. But under the new covenant, God promises that if we seek His kingdom first and His righteousness, He will give us something even better: Everything that we need for life on this earth (*Matthew 6:33*; see also *2 Peter 1:4*). The Bible clearly teaches that riches are both deceitful and uncertain (*Matthew 13:22*; *1 Timothy 6:17*). So it is dangerous to desire riches or to long to have more and more money (*1 Timothy 6:10*). But God's promise is something far more glorious: He will always give us "all that we need, according to his riches in glory IN Christ Jesus" (*Philippians 4:19*).

Do you find you cannot make ends meet with the salary that you earn? Since God draws everyone's financial boundaries, it is impossible for Him not to give His children enough for their earthly needs. Your lack must then be because the blessing of God is not on your life. Maybe you are lazy, or wasting money, or living in a selfish way, violating God's laws. If you are rich towards God, God will be rich towards you as well.

Let me tell you the good news of the gospel: It is not God's will that His children should live with constant financial lack in their earthly lives. However high the cost of living may be, those who seek the kingdom of God and His righteousness first in their lives will always find that their earthly needs are met.

If that does not happen, we would have to say that Jesus was a liar – for that is what He clearly promised (*Matthew 6:33*).

Jesus became poor – so that we might be rich. So we need never live with a lack in our lives. We need have no fear about the future – either for ourselves or for our children. Jesus has purchased the provision of every earthly need for us and our family-members – on the cross.

Unfortunately, money-loving preachers (especially in the last thirty years or so) have exaggerated and misunderstood this truth and turned it into an excuse to preach a "prosperity-gospel" – teaching that Jesus came to make us wealthy millionaires. That is a falsehood and a misrepresentation of the truth. God has not promised us wealth in the new covenant, but something far better – all that we need.

So be free from all your fears, dear brother and sister. Jesus has already become poor for you on the cross. There is no need for you to live with constant financial lack in your lives any more. You can always have all that you need. Claim your birthright in the gospel.

3. Jesus Became a Curse in Order to Make Us a Blessing

"Christ redeemed us from the curse of the Law, having become a curse for us – in order that the blessing of Abraham might come to us, so that we might receive the promise of the Spirit through faith" (*Galatians 3:13, 14*).

Christ became a curse for us, so that we might receive the blessing of Abraham – that is, the promise of the Holy Spirit.

The curse for not keeping the Law is described in *Deuteronomy 28:15–68* as confusion, incurable sicknesses, plagues, constant failure, blindness, madness, no rest or peace of mind, being exploited by others, children being captured by the enemy (Satan), abject poverty etc.

The good news of the gospel is that because Jesus has already become a curse for us, none of these curses of the Law need touch us any more. That itself would have been good news. But there is more. We can have instead, the blessing with which God blessed Abraham.

Note that the blessing we are promised in that verse, is NOT the blessing of the Law (described in *Deuteronomy 28:1–14*), which consists mainly of material prosperity and many children. No. We are promised something better – the blessing of Abraham.

The blessing with which God blessed Abraham is described thus in *Genesis 12:2, 3*: "I will bless you...so you shall be a blessing... and in you all the families of the earth shall be blessed". This is the blessing that Christ has purchased for us on the cross through His becoming a curse for us. He wants to bless us and make us a blessing to every person that we come across on earth, all our life.

> This blessing (the verse tells us) comes to us through receiving the Holy Spirit. Jesus described the Holy Spirit as a well of water springing up within us and BLESSING US (*John 4:14*), and then as rivers of water flowing out through us and BLESSING OTHERS (*John 7:37–39*).

If you seek to receive the Holy Spirit by trying to make yourself worthy, you will never receive Him. There is no difference between that and Simon the magician offering money to Peter to receive the Spirit's power (*Acts 8:18–23*). Peter told Simon to repent. And you must repent too – for imagining that you can buy the Holy Spirit with your good works.

> Come to Jesus as you are and confess your unworthiness, and receive the Spirit by faith, JUST BECAUSE JESUS BECAME A CURSE FOR YOU – and not because you are worthy.

How has your own life been in the past? Have you found that whatever you have put your hand to has been a failure? Have you found that the words that you have spoken to others have only brought confusion and chaos? Have you found frustration and depression and gloom and loss everywhere you have turned.

Here is the good news of the gospel, dear brother and sister. You can be free from all of that permanently. Christ has taken the curse of the Law so that you might never receive it. Not only can you be free from those curses, you can now be a blessing to others.

The Lord's promise to even the worst sinner living in sin and failure today is:

> *"Even as you have been a CURSE in times past, you can be a BLESSING to others in times to come"* (Zechariah 8:13).

Perhaps you have been a curse to others in the past, by polluting everyone you've met, with your criticisms, your gossiping and your backbiting. Have you been a spreader of spiritual plague everywhere you have gone? Things can be different from now on. You can be a spreader of spiritual healing and blessing to others now. God can make rivers of living water flow through you, so that wherever you go, others are healed and blessed through the Holy Spirit working through you (*Ezekiel 47:8, 9*).

This is the will of God that we should be a BLESSING to every family we meet on the face of the earth. But you must believe God's Word and claim your birthright in Christ. Satan has robbed you of this for so long. You must now believe that since Jesus has already become a curse for you, no curse can touch you henceforth. You are going to be a blessing to your family, to your neighbours and to the church. Hallelujah!

We read about King David in *2 Samuel 6* that after a busy day in which he had been serving God, he then returned home "to bless his family" (*verse 20*). What beautiful words! He had been dancing the whole day before the ark when it was being brought into Jerusalem (*verse 14*), and was undoubtedly tired. He had also been busy blessing the people (*verses 18, 19*). But he did not forget his wife at home. He went home and blessed her too – even though she was a wicked, nagging wife (*verses 20–22*).

What a wonderful example for every head of the family to follow! Even if you had to dance to the tune of your boss the whole day at work, you can still return home in the evening to bless your family, instead of coming home in a foul mood and bringing a bad spirit into your home.

Since Jesus has defeated Satan also on the cross, and stripped his armour from him completely, Satan too has no right over any part of our lives. Satan is now like a helpless thief who has lost all his weapons. We however are now armed with every heavenly weapon against him. So we don't ever have to be afraid of him. We are commanded to resist Satan in Jesus' Name. The promise of God is that Satan will flee from us.

> We cannot any more be affected by black magic or witchcraft or any evil that anyone may seek to do against us. We are living under the blessing of God in Christ. No evil can touch us anymore, as long as we remain IN CHRIST. God Who "turned the curse into a blessing" for Israel years ago, can turn every curse into a blessing for us too (*Deuteronomy 23:5*).

If there has been a curse upon your family, because of the way your parents lived, or because they worshipped idols or dabbled with the occult, you can break that curse in Jesus' Name and drive it out of your life – permanently. It can have no power over you from this day onwards. Jesus has become a curse for you. Take the blessing He offers you NOW.

When people curse us, Jesus told us to bless them in return (*Luke 6:28*). This is our calling – to be a blessing even to those who are evil towards us (See *1 Peter 3:9*). This is why we are anointed with the Holy Spirit – so that as Jesus "went about doing good" (*Acts 10:38*), we too can go around doing good and blessing people everywhere. No-one who comes in touch with you in future, will be polluted or hurt by your words, as in past days. Instead, they will be blessed – and blessed abundantly.

Every blessing in the heavenly places is ours in Christ. We must first of all believe that in our hearts. Then we must confess it with our mouths. The Bible says that "with the heart man believes...and with the mouth he confesses resulting in salvation (and deliverance)" (*Romans 10:10*).

It is not enough that you believe all these truths in your heart. Confess them with your mouth to Satan, and be an overcomer always. In that way, "by the word of your testimony", you will put Satan to flight, and be a blessing to others around you (*Revelation 12:11*). Yes, EVEN YOU can be a blessing to every person you meet – not because of what you are or what you have done, but because of what Jesus has done for you.

When Paul was going to Rome, he told the Christians there, "I KNOW that when I come to you, I will come in the FULLNESS of the blessing of CHRIST" (*Romans 15:29*). He was absolutely certain that he would be an overflowing blessing to them in Rome, in Jesus' Name.

> Every disciple of Jesus can make that confession and believe that God will make him a blessing to everyone he meets. I have claimed that as my birthright in Christ, for many years now, and believed that everywhere I go, I WILL go in the fullness of the blessing of Christ – not because of what I am, but because Jesus became a curse for me on the cross.

We go to God now in Jesus' Name – in Jesus' merit – and not our own: In His Name Who became sin for us, we become the righteousness of God. In His Name Who became poor for us, we are rich forever. In His Name Who became a curse for us, we can be a blessing to others forever.

5

That Which was from the Beginning

"What was from the beginning, what we have heard, what we have seen with our eyes, what we beheld and our hands handled, concerning the Word of Life – and the life was manifested, and we have seen and bear witness and proclaim to you the eternal life, which was with the Father and was manifested to us – what we have seen and heard we proclaim to you also, that you also may have fellowship with us; and indeed our fellowship is with the Father, and with His Son Jesus Christ" (1 John 1:1–3).

The letters of the apostles in the New Testament, although all inspired by the Holy Spirit, nevertheless display the level of maturity of the apostle at the time when he wrote that letter.

In this sense, we can say that *1 John* would manifest the maximum maturity, because John wrote this towards the end of his life – when he was over 90 years old, and after having carefully observed the development of the church and of Christianity over a period of 60 years.

And what does John speak about?

What is his burden for the Christians in the various churches?

In his whole letter he never speaks even once about the gift of tongues or of healing or of any spiritual gift or even of evangelism! All these are good and necessary – but none of them are primary.

John speaks about those things which were from the beginning – those things which were with God from before time began – LIFE and FELLOWSHIP.

What God had from all eternity was the Divine life of love. And between Father, Son & Holy Spirit there existed a blessed and perfect fellowship of love. This is John's theme and burden. This is what he longs to partake of more and more and this is what he wants all believers to partake of more and more.

This is the ultimate goal of God – that we may partake of His nature and become one as the Father and Jesus are one (*John 17:3, 21*).

In the beginning, there was no preaching, no songbooks, no New-Testament-pattern church, and not even any doctrine. All of these came subsequently and were brought forth for a purpose, for a time. But there was only life and fellowship in the beginning.

In the same way, in the future, in eternity, once again there will be no preaching or songbooks or healing – but only life and fellowship.

So we see that at the beginning of time and at the end of time, only life and fellowship existed/will exist. All other things are only for this in-between period in which we are living right now.

To speak in tongues, for example, is an edifying experience. But we won't be needing that gift in heaven in eternity, because we will not have any limitations in our communication with God there. Preaching is a very necessary thing here on earth. But it won't be necessary in eternity.

Even victory over sin is only for a period – during the time when we are in the flesh and can be tempted. Once we reach heaven, we will no longer even be tempted. In the beginning, it was not "victory over sin" that God had, but a Divine life of perfect love!!

This is why we must see clearly that life and fellowship are the two most essential things needed in the church today. If we don't have these, then whatever else we may have in our church, we have failed God.

Life

It is the life of God that must be found in our midst primarily – that life of love that always seeks to serve and bless others, and seeks their good. God's every action is designed to bless others. This is one of the primary characteristics of the Divine life.

In heaven, when we hear someone say something or see someone do something, we won't have any question in our minds as to their motive. The motive will only be to bless us. How wonderful if our fellowship on earth is like that now.

Among the unconverted, "the poison of snakes is under their lips" (*Romans 3:13*), and they speak words that are designed to sting and hurt others. But such a poison should never be found in the mouth of anyone in the church. In the church, everyone's words must be only to bless.

The Holy Spirit has come to bring the atmosphere of heaven into our hearts. Under the old covenant, they could only have laws that enabled them to live a life that was very righteous compared to the life of the rest of humanity. But now we have more than just Divine laws to guide us, we have the Divine life itself to govern our actions.

Heaven is heaven because the presence of God is there. Where God is, there is heaven. Where God is not present, that is hell. Here on earth the presence of God is still found everywhere. And that is why we find some goodness even in unconverted people. But in hell, those very same people will be quite different. There their selfishness and their pride will be unrestrained, and they will be known as they really are, without the restraining influences of God's goodness.

In heaven there is also blessed fellowship. There is no lording it over others there. Everyone is a servant of others. Those like Lucifer who want to rule over others will never be found in heaven, for his attitude was, "It is better to rule in hell than to serve in heaven." That is the essence of the spirit of Satan – the desire to rule over others.

Therefore husbands who rule their wives like tyrants, and wives who do not submit to their husbands are creating a hell in their own homes.

Those brothers who lord it over others in their churches bring hell into their churches too, and build Babylon.

Heaven has a totally different spirit, because God is a Father there. He does not dominate people, but lovingly shepherds them and serves them. That is the nature we are to partake of.

We are promised crowns in heaven if we are faithful now. What does that mean? Does it mean that we will then rule people. No, not at all. It means that we who had a longing to serve our brothers here on earth, but could not do it perfectly because of various limitations, will find all those limitations gone in heaven, and we will be able to serve others perfectly. Thus the longing of our hearts will be fulfilled.

The greatest Person in heaven will be Jesus Himself and He will be the greatest servant of all. His spirit will forever be the spirit of service.

The church has been placed by God on earth to be a little sample of heaven, for others to taste of. It is something like a biscuit-company sending you a small sample of their biscuits and asking you to taste it and see whether you want more.

God also has sent us to earth to show forth the values of His kingdom to others, so that they may be attracted to Him. What taste do others get from us?

When Jesus walked on this earth, people saw and tasted a little sample of the life of heaven. They saw His compassion, His consideration for others, His purity and His selfless love and humility. Heaven is like that. God is like that – full of compassion for sinners and for those who have failed in life.

At the same time Jesus revealed the Father as One who was ruthless with religious hypocrites, and with those who make money in the name of God, and sends them to hell. Heaven won't have a single person who pretends to be holy, but who has no mercy on others.

When heaven comes down into our churches, our churches must manifest this kind of life. When Jesus (the Second Person of the Trinity) came down to earth He needed a body to manifest the life of God.

Now that the Holy Spirit (the Third person of the Trinity) has come down, he needs bodies too, to manifest the life of heaven in. If Jesus had been on earth without a body, think what limitation there would have been in His earthly life. No-one would have been able to know what God was like then. Thank God that Jesus had a body.

This is why it is so precious that we have bodies – because through them the life of God can be manifested to others by the Holy Spirit.

In the church, others must see this life of God. They must not see in just a set of doctrines or even a lot of zeal to preach. No. There must see much more than that. They must see the life of God's kingdom. Otherwise we have failed God as a church.

Even though our actions may not be perfect, our motives must be perfect. We may not be able to serve and bless others perfectly. But our motive must always be to glorify God and bless the others.

There are sisters in the churches who still haven't got rid of the flirtatious spirit that they had when they were unconverted and worldly. They still raise their eyebrows in a certain way, and toss their head in certain way – habits that they acquired from watching film-actresses in the movies in the old days. Such sisters are a hindrance to the witness of the church. These mannerisms will not disappear the moment you are converted. They will disappear only if you hate them, and work out your own salvation from them.

It is this life that makes us pure. If we don't have it, we will only be religious. It is good for us to examine ourselves constantly to see whether we are only religious or truly spiritual.

Here is one area where we could all examine ourselves:

How many of us who are married would honestly pray this prayer: "Lord, don't make me attractive in any way – physically, intellectually or otherwise – to anyone other than my marriage-partner". That would be the sincere heart-cry of every Christian man and woman who longs for total inward purity.

What a shame it is when married Christian men and women still seek to be attractive to others of the opposite sex. If such brothers and sisters come and sit in our midst, they must be made to feel uncomfortable every time they come to a meeting. That is our calling as a church – to make half-hearted, compromising believers uncomfortable in every meeting. We don't drive anybody out – unless they commit outward sin. But the fire in the church must make every religious humbug uncomfortable until he either repents or gets offended and leaves the church. These religious humbugs may fool the vast multitude in the church. But the elders must not be fooled.

Prophetic ministry in the church will make people uncomfortable who do not long for the atmosphere of heaven in their lives. Let us pray that we shall have such a ministry in our churches in every meeting.

There is a spirit of adultery in the world. A whole host of unclean spirits have flooded the world, especially in the last fifty years, like the frogs that flooded ancient Egypt (Compare *Revelation 16:13* with *Exodus 8:3–6*). There are frogs in the bedrooms, frogs in the newspapers, frogs on the streets, frogs everywhere.

We hope that when we come to the church there won't be any frogs there. But Satan will send them there too. But it is our calling to cast out these unclean spirits, so that the spirit in the church is one of purity. There are young people and even older married people who have this spirit of the frog in them. Many of these are very zealous in religious activity. But they are impure.

We must all be careful. When you brothers are speaking to a woman or even to a sister, if you sense an unclean spirit (a frog) there, beware. Avoid her as you would avoid the plague, lest you destroy yourself finally.

Or conversely, if you sisters see impurity in the eyes of any man, or even in someone who calls himself a brother – a frog in the eye – then avoid him at any cost, if you would remain pure.

In ancient Egypt, in the land of Goshen (where the Israelites lived) there were no frogs. Our churches must be like that – free from impurity and filled with the atmosphere of heaven.

The measure in which you can bring the life of heaven into your church, determines the measure in which you are useful to the church. And the measure in which you bring any spirit other than the spirit of heaven into the church, in that measure you are an agent of Satan, hindering the work of God in your local church.

Fellowship

When we have the life of God, it will lead to fellowship.

The Father, Son and Holy Spirit had glorious fellowship with each other from all eternity. There was never any competition or jealousy among them at any time. All three Persons in the Godhead knew from all eternity what their ministries in relation to man would be.

It was not after Adam fell, that the Three Persons of the Godhead decided what to do. No. They knew the end from the beginning. And so Christ's death on the cross was in their mind from all eternity. The "Lamb was slain from the foundation of the world" (*Revelation 13:8*).

The coming of the Holy Spirit to earth was also known from all eternity. The fact that the Father would be the One to Whom the Son and the Holy Spirit would submit was also known from all eternity. Yet their differing ministries did not cause any difficulties between them.

It never disturbed the Son that He would be subject to the Father for all eternity to come (*1 Corinthians 15:28*).

Many wives find it difficult to be subject to their husbands even for 365 days. Many brothers find it a great problem to submit to older and wiser brothers. Yet the Son of God had no problem taking a low position.

That is one result of fellowship.

Where there is fellowship, there will be no competition or jealousy. Where there is no fellowship however, brothers will be constantly itching to be elders. Some, although willing to submit, are waiting for the day when they will become elders. This is the spirit of Lucifer.

Consider the ministry of the Holy Spirit. His is the most invisible of all the ministries in the Godhead. He encourages and helps in a silent, invisible way, without even wanting recognition or credit for His work. He is quite content for people to praise the Father and Jesus alone, and to be left out of the picture altogether. What a beautiful ministry.

What does it mean then to be filled with such a Spirit? It must mean that we will be like Him, content to have a ministry like His – silent, invisible, receiving no credit, and content for the credit to go to others.

Are we indeed filled with this Spirit?

Many who claim to be "filled with the Holy Spirit" today however seek such prominence for themselves through the exercise of their gifts on Christian platforms, promote themselves, and seek for money for themselves. All this is anything but the work of the Holy Spirit. All this is the work of some other spirit counterfeiting the Holy Spirit, and it is our duty in the church to expose such counterfeit and deception.

Is it because the life of Jesus and of the Holy Spirit is any less than that of the Father that they submit to Him. No. Their life is exactly the same in every way. They submit because it is the joy of each member of the Godhead to submit to each other. That is part of the life of God.

Is it because a sister's life is inferior to her husband's that God asks her to submit to her husband. No. It is because her ministry is different. How wonderful if all sisters could see this glory of Jesus and the Holy Spirit. But alas, there are very few sisters who have seen this glory.

If a sister has not seen her calling to submit to the man as the head in the church, there is every danger that she will become a Jezebel in that church (*Revelation 2:20*). And the Lord will then rebuke the elders in such a church, like He rebuked the elder in Thyatira – for the fault is always with the elders, when a Jezebel is allowed to flourish in a church. Jezebels bring the spirit of Lucifer into a church and the elders must be strong to drive that spirit right out, as soon as it begins to manifest itself. The woman herself does not have be driven out. But her spirit must be brought into subjection to Divinely-appointed leadership in the church. We don't need dictators as elders, but we do need firm fathers.

If the spirit of heaven is to be found in a church, then we have to be firm to resist every manifestation of the spirit of hell.

Wherever this genuine life of God is found, there will always be found this quality of fellowship too between the brothers and sisters. And wherever such a quality of fellowship is not found, we can say with absolute certainty that the genuine life of God is not there. All that such brothers and sisters. All they must be having is religion.

> The fellowship that is found in the Godhead is what the Lord wants to reproduce in every church everywhere.

Jesus valued that fellowship with the Father more than anything else. It was when He knew that that fellowship would be broken for three hours on the cross that He cried out in Gethsemane, asking if there wasn't any other way to save the human race without His having to pay such a tremendous cost.

We cannot fully realise what a great cost that was to Jesus, because none of us have ever valued the fellowship of the Father like He did. We see that after that extended time of prayer, Jesus was willing to lose even His most valued possession (fellowship with the Father), in order to save our souls. That is where we see the greatness of His love for us.

Many see the love of Jesus in His being willing to suffer physically and to die on the cross. But that physical suffering was not even one-millionth of what He suffered when His fellowship with the Father was broken because of our sin, for those three dark hours on Calvary's cross. One day, when we see Him face to face, we will see that that was the greatest manifestation of His love for us.

It was because Jesus valued fellowship with the Father so much that He "cried with loud crying and tears" to the Father to save Him from death(spiritual death). The only thing that Jesus ever wanted to be saved from was a break of fellowship with the Father. He was willing to lose everything else. Everything else was utter garbage for Him.

It is only when we consider everything as garbage (and even as human dung) compared to fellowship with the Father, that we will find that fellowship with the Father that the apostle John wrote of in his first epistle. It is such fellowship with the Father that in turn brings to true fellowship with each other in the church.

Another aspect of heaven is seen in *Revelation 4:10*. There we read that the elders "cast their crowns down before God". No-one but Jesus will have crown on His head in heaven. All the rest of us will be ordinary brothers and sisters there. There are no special brothers or sisters in heaven. Those who seek to be special brothers or sisters in the church bring the atmosphere of hell into the church.

We will also never boast of anything when we stand before the Father. Everything that we have, we will cast down before Him. In heaven, no-one will ever say "This is mine", concerning anything he may have (not even concerning the crown that he received).

When the atmosphere of heaven begins to pervade our churches, we too will never again say concerning anything that we may have, "This is mine". Everything will be considered as God's and therefore as available freely for the spread of God's kingdom on earth.

Every miser and every selfish person who lives for himself and his own gain is under the control of Satan.

It is a great grief to God's heart that there is no fellowship between millions of His children on earth. So many have bitterness against others. Others are self-righteous Pharisees who imagine that God has chosen only them and not the others.

God is distressed with both these groups of His children – for they are all frustrating His purpose for the church.

> The most valuable brother and sister in any church is the one who can bring the atmosphere of heaven into a church and who can build fellowship between the brothers and sisters in that church.

And this need not necessarily be the elder brother. All of us have the opportunity to become such valuable brothers and sisters.

Think if there is a brother or a sister in a church, who whenever he/she comes into a meeting or into a home, is like a pure breeze from heaven blowing through the room. What a precious brother/sister such a person is! Even if he stops by and visits you for just five minutes, you feel refreshed. You feel as if heaven came into your home for five minutes! He may not have given you a sermon or even a word of revelation from the Scriptures. But he was so pure. He was not moody or gloomy and had no complaints against anyone. Such a brother may never speak first in a meeting (as many have the lust to do). He may speak fifteenth in every meeting perhaps, and that too for just three minutes. But those will be three minutes of heaven in the meeting!

Since the world is full of complainers and murmurers, it is so refreshing to meet a brother like that. It is just like having a bath, on a hot, sticky day! That is the type of brother/sister that we all should long to be like. Jesus was like that and He wants to make us like that too.

How sad it is that instead of doing that, many brothers and sisters are going around creating more problems wherever they go. They go around separating the brothers and sisters from each other by their gossiping. These are the servants and agents of Lucifer.

We are called to live with each other exactly as the Father, Son and Holy Spirit lived with each other. They were not preaching to each other back there in eternity past, but having fellowship. We too are not called to preach to each other, but to have fellowship.

That is heaven. And that is where the new and living way is meant to lead us to. I fear that many of us have got so taken up with the way that we have never arrived at the destination – fellowship with the Father.

Think if you were coming for a conference to Bangalore, and on the way you got so taken up with admiring the road that leads to Bangalore, that you never reach Bangalore at all. And think if a number of you sat on the road halfway to Bangalore and began to share with each other the virtues of the road, instead of traveling on it. You would never reach Bangalore at all.

That is a fair description of what goes on in many churches today. They are always talking about the new and living way through the flesh – about putting the flesh to death and bearing the dying of Jesus etc., etc., – without realising that this has value only because it leads us inside the veil (*Hebrews 10:20*) to meet and fellowship with the Father.

Jesus was never taken up with the cross itself in His daily life. He did not enjoy the cross. We are told that He endured it (*Hebrews 12:2*). The joy for Jesus was what was "set before Him" – fellowship with the Father. This is the joy that we must be taken up with too.

Way back in the beginning, when only God existed, there was no flesh to be put to death, and that is why John does not even mention it in His epistle – not because it is not important, but because that is not his theme. John emphasises what was from the beginning – life and fellowship. Let us emphasise these too in our churches at all times.

6

Married to Christ

"If you abide in My word, you shall know the truth and the truth shall make you free" (John 8:32).

Every bondage in our lives comes because in some measure we do not know the truth. This may be either because we have not heard the truth at all or because we have not paid careful attention to it. It could also be possible that we have heard the truth, but understood it wrongly. All feelings of condemnation too are the result of not knowing the truth.

Many young people especially are hesitant to become disciples of Jesus, because they feel they will not be able to hold out (endure) until the end. And so they think that if they make a public confession of being a disciple of Jesus, and then slip up and fall in some way, perhaps by losing their temper, or by lusting, they will be mocked by others and then regret that they ever confessed the Lord publicly at all. Thus the devil keeps them unconverted forever.

But no believer is perfect. No-one on earth can claim that he is walking at all times as Jesus walked. "He who abides in Christ must walk as Jesus walked" (*1 John 2:6*). That is certainly our goal. But yet we all stumble now and then as we press on toward that goal. James, the chief elder in the church at Jerusalem, admitted that he too stumbled occasionally ("WE ALL stumble" – *James 3:2*).

But what should we do when we slip up or stumble? Get up and continue to run.

No-one quits school, just because he failed once in a Chemistry test. No. He will attend special classes and seek to pass in the next test.

When we fail, let us be honest about it and confess our failure to God and mourn about it. God is not populating heaven with perfect people but with honest people.

In my own life, the promise of Jesus in *John 6:37* ("He who comes to me I will certainly not cast out") has been like an anchor for 36 years now. For many years prior to that, I had been tossed about, wondering whether Jesus had accepted me or not. I must have asked the Lord to come into my heart a hundred times in my teenage years. But I always wondered whether He had actually come into my heart or not. One day in simple faith in this promise of the Lord, and without any special feelings at all, I said to the Lord, "Lord I believe You have accepted me." My assurance has been unshaken since that day.

But that promise applies not only when we come to the Lord the first time. It applies as long as we live on this earth. I find that I need this verse today, just as much as I did when I was first born again.

Maybe you did not get time to read your Bible this morning. Or perhaps you failed in some other way. Don't you think you need to come to Jesus again? Do you think He will reject you? Never. Come to the Lord and He will not only accept you but also lead you to a higher degree of glory than you have experienced thus far.

But we must not forget that we receive from the Lord "according to the measure of our FAITH". Faith puts all of us at the same level. If the Lord had said that we would receive according to the measure of our knowledge, or our wealth, or our goodness, then intelligent and wealthy people would have had an advantage over the others. Those who are naturally good in a human way would also have had an advantage over those who have a naturally difficult temperament. That's why God has made faith the way, because that puts us all at the same level.

Let me illustrate what having faith really means. Consider two bridges across a river – one a rickety wooden bridge made of weak sticks and the other a strong concrete bridge supported by many pillars placed into the river-bed? Why is it that you can walk with confidence over the concrete bridge but would be afraid to step on the rickety wooden bridge? It has nothing to do with your ability to believe. It has only to do with the type of bridge you are walking on.

In the same way, our faith is to be in Jesus Christ who is like a solid concrete bridge, and not in our own ability to believe. Even if we are weak, we can walk across, because we have faith in the bridge and not in our abilities. The trouble with many of us is that our faith is very often founded on our own faith – and our faith is as unreliable as a rickety wooden bridge!

Such faith would be equivalent to working up a strong mental feeling of confidence in ourselves and then trying to cross the river on the rickety bridge. Half way across the bridge, the bridge would collapse and we would drown. That is what happens when we have faith in our own faith. But what difficulty is there in having faith in the strong, concrete bridge. It does not matter how turbulent the water in the river is. We can still cross the river over that strong bridge, without any fear.

Or consider another example. When you walk on a road that goes under a railway track, do you ever worry that the bridge might collapse and the train might fall on you and crush you to death? Do you have to be a great man of faith to go under such a rail-bridge? No. Hundreds of people walk underneath it daily. Their faith is not in themselves, but in the strength of that bridge.

Faith is as simple a matter as that. When your faith is in Jesus Christ, you don't look at your own faith – YOU LOOK AT JESUS.

How many there are who insult God by fearing that the devil might harm them in one way or another? Therefore they never accomplish what God wants them to for fear paralyses them. They could be compared to a man standing forever beside that concrete bridge, fearing that he might fall into the river. Thousands cross the bridge fearlessly, with no more faith than he has. But since he does not look at the bridge, but at his own faith, he is paralysed. And so he never reaches the other side.

Do you see now why faith is so important – and so simple? The Lord is asking you now, "Will you trust Me? If you do, I can set you free from every bondage"

The Christian life is essentially very, very simple. Many of us have misunderstood what God expects of us. We know we can come to Jesus freely, initially. But after we are saved, we feel somehow that the Lord expects us to be perfect before we come to Him now. But He still assures us saying, "If anyone comes to me I will certainly not cast him out."

Remember that – wherever you go. Whatever the difficulty or problem that you may be facing anywhere, tell the Lord.

"Lord I believe You will never cast me out. I come to You." Trust Him and see the miracles that God will do for you.

To those who have been hesitant for a long time to make a real commitment to the Lord, because of the fear that you may not endure until the end, I say: Tell the Lord that you want to be His disciple. You may fail. But if you fail, get up and continue to run. If you fail in a test, do it a second time. If you fail again, do it a third time – or the twentieth time – or even the ten-thousandth time. But don't let the devil make you quit school. Be determined to pass. I assure you that you will pass.

Jesus taught us to forgive others 490 times in a single day (See *Matthew 18:21, 22* along with *Luke 17:4*). Do you think He wont forgive us also that many times in a single day? It would be impossible for Jesus to ask us to forgive others 490 times every day and not forgive us that many times Himself. Then let us trust Him totally.

Two Types of Bondage

Let us look at the story of Lazarus being raised from the dead and see TWO types of bondage that most believers are in.

First of all, Lazarus was in bondage to death. He was so dead that a terrible stench was coming out of his body. This was so bad that they did not even want to open the grave (*verse 39*). But Jesus set him free from that bondage.

Secondly, after Lazarus came out of the grave, He was in the bondage of his grave-clothes. But Jesus set him free from that bondage too.

So we see three stages in Lazarus' deliverance:

First stage: Dead and stinking
Second stage: Alive but bound with grave clothes
Third stage: Totally free

All of us are in one of these three stages today.

As you read further, don't hesitate to roll the stone away and to acknowledge your true condition before God. You don't have to confess your sins to men. But be honest before God.

Because they exposed the stench that day at Bethany, we read in the next chapter that "the house was filled with the fragrance of the perfume." (*John 12:3*).

That is a wonderful picture of what the Lord can do in our lives too. Even when things are so bad that we want to cover them up, the Lord can change things. It did not take long there in Bethany. And it need not take long in your life either.

Then Lazarus could invite others to come and see that the Lord had done for him. No-one in that home could take the credit for that. The Lord had done it all.

We read in *John 11:3* that when Jesus heard that Lazarus was sick, he stayed for two more days at the same time.

What was Jesus waiting for?

He was waiting for Lazarus to stop struggling. He was waiting for the time when Lazarus would not be able to lift even his little finger. He was waiting for total death to enter in.

That is God's way and we find this principle in all of God's deal-ings with men, throughout the Bible – from Genesis to Revelation.

The world says, "God helps those who help themselves." But that isn't true, just like a lot of other worldly proverbs are not true. The truth is, "God helps those who CANNOT help themselves."

It was when Lazarus was thoroughly helpless and dead that Jesus came. When we reach the place where we feel our case is absolutely hopeless, it is then that the Lord steps in to help us.

Have you come to the place where you feel that it is impossible for you to live according to the standard of life proclaimed in the Bible? If so, you are very close to deliverance.

Many misunderstand what we actually teach, because they have not heard us first hand. Some imagine that our primary message is related to things like not having a TV set in the home, not wearing ornaments, sisters not being employed outside the home etc. But they are totally mistaken. Such things are so unim-portant, as far as I am concerned, that they are not even found at the bottom of my list of God's standards for holy living. God's standard is the life of Jesus – and that is an inward matter and has nothing to do with any of the things just mentioned.

Why is your life not progressing then towards perfection? The answer is: Because you are still struggling.

Jesus is waiting for you to stop your struggling and to die.

A Tale of Three Marriages

In *Romans 6 and 7*, the Holy Spirit shows us how the Lord sets us free today in the same way as He set Lazarus free. Here are the three stages for us:

> *First stage:* Dead and unable to do anything
> *Second stage:* Born again but bound by the grave clothes of the Law
> *Third stage:* Totally free

When we were born into the world, we were all born married – married to what the Bible calls "the old man"!!

"The old man" is different from "the flesh".

The flesh consists of many lusts. They could be likened to a gang of robbers that come to rob our house. They don't live inside our house (our heart). They come from outside.

We are not married to the flesh, but to the old man.

The "old man" however is a terrible husband. He ill treats us and beats us up every day. And in addition, each time the gang of robbers come (the lusts in the flesh) to the house, the old man opens the door and invites them in to beat us up and to molest us. Here is a husband who not only beats up his wife himself, but allows even others to come in and molest her.

Which woman would ever want to be married to such a man? Any wife would only be too happy to be free of such a husband.

But how can she ever get rid of him? She may want to be married to Christ. But the law says that as long as her first husband is alive, she cannot marry another man. If while "the old man" is living, she wants to be married to Christ as well, she would "become an adulteress" (*Romans 7:3*). This is how Babylon the harlot (adulteress) is built – through "believers" who live with their old husband, the "old man".

In such a situation, we are as helpless to deliver ourselves as the Israelites in Egypt were. We can only cry out to God. The Israelites cried out to God in Egypt and God heard their cry and liberated them. God can liberate us too.

There is only one way by which God can deliver us from this marriage to the old man, and that is by killing him.

And that is what God did on the cross.

In *Romans 6:6* we read "our old man was crucified with Christ."

This is what we testify to in baptism (*Romans 6:4*). Jesus not only took our sins upon Himself when He died on the cross. He put our "old man" to death on that cross too. That leaves us free now to marry Christ.

This is the good news of the gospel – that God has killed your old man and now invites you to be married to Christ.

One would think that all our problems would now be solved. But they are not. Most believers (in fact over 99% of them), after being freed from their marriage to the old man, then go and marry "The Law", imagining that they are marrying Christ!!

This is what the first part of *Romans 7* deals with.

The Law is different from the old man, in that he is a good, morally upright husband. This is why we mistake him for Christ.

But the Law is a very demanding husband. He expects perfection in every area.

He demands that the wife must keep the home absolutely spick and span. Books and clothes and shoes must all be kept in their proper places. There must not be a speck of dust found anywhere in the house. The food must be ready on time – breakfast at 8.00 a.m. and not one minute late. Lunch must be ready at 1.00 p.m. and not at 1.01 p.m. The food must have the perfect proportion of salt and spices. etc., etc.

At the same time, he will not life one finger to help you with your work. He will not give you a hand in the kitchen or anywhere else. When he walks into the house, everything must be ready – and perfect.

This husband (the Law) never beats you or hurts you. Neither can you find any fault with any of his demands – for they are all righteous. Such is God's Law.

But how many women would like to be married to such a man??

Consider the fate of a woman married to such a man. She cannot divorce him. at the same time she cannot marry Christ, for a woman cannot have two husbands. And the worst part of the bad news of being married to "the Law" is that unlike "the old man", this husband is perfectly healthy. He looks as if he will never die in ten thousand years.

God cannot kill "the Law", for it is absolutely perfect. "The old man" was wicked and so could be killed righteously. But not "the Law", for he has never done anything wrong.

Is there a solution then to this new problem?

Yes, praise God, there is, for there is nothing impossible with God.

What does the Lord do?

He kills the wife!!

Since the Law cannot die, *Romans 7:4* says, "YOU (the wife) were made to die to the Law".

That is God's way of liberating us from this second marriage.

We were placed "in Christ" when He died on the cross, and we died with Him.

If it is difficult for you to understand how you could possible have existed "in Christ" 2000 years ago, then look at *Hebrews 7:9, 10*. There the Holy Spirit tell us that Levi paid tithes to Melchizedek, because Levi was "in Abraham" when Abraham paid tithes to Melchizedek. The Holy Spirit's argument runs like this: Since Levi was Jacob's son, a little bit of Levi was "in Jacob", and since Jacob was Isaac's son, a little bit of Levi must have been "in Isaac" too. And since Isaac was Abraham's son, a little bit of Levi was definitely "in Abraham" too!

In the same way, long before you and I were born, we existed in the mind of God. We were there in the beginning in God's mind and God put us all in Christ, so that He could have mercy on all of us. And so, when Jesus died years ago, on the cross, we died with Him.

All marriages are only "until death do us part". So, once we are dead, the marriage is annulled and finished. We are thus freed from this husband who demanded perfection, but who never helped us in any way to attain it. What a wonderful way God has made for us to escape out of this marriage.

Romans 7:4 (KJV) tells us that we are made to die to the Law in order that we might now "be married to Christ who was raised from the dead."

The Lord has now raised us up from the dead, so that we might be married to Christ – at last! What a glorious message the gospel is!!

Think of the folly of people who still want to be married either to the old man or to the Law.

Now what are Jesus' standards like? Are they lower than those of the Law? Does He permit us to keep our house (our heart) unclean and dirty? No. In fact, His standards are much higher.

If the Law said that we were not to commit murder, Jesus says that we must not even be angry. If the Law said that we were not to commit adultery, Jesus says that we must not even lust in our hearts.

To use the earlier illustration: Like the Law, Jesus wants the breakfast to be ready promptly at 8.00 a.m. too. But if the law would not condone one minute's delay, Jesus does not condone even one second's delay!!

Does this mean that we have jumped out of the frying pan into the fire, and are now married to an even greater perfectionist than the Law?

No. There is a world of difference between Jesus and the Law. Jesus' standards may be higher than those of the Law, but He comes along to help us in all our tasks. He says, "Let us do everything together. Let us clean the house together. Let us put the cloths and the shoes in their proper place together. Let us wash the clothes together.

But what if we are such total failures that we are not only unable to have breakfast ready by 8.00 a.m., but are unable to have it ready even by 4.00 p.m.? What will the Lord do then? He will still not reproach us. He will say, 'All right. Let us start from there and work on it so that you and I make breakfast ready by 3.45 p.m. tomorrow. Then we'll improve on it still further the next day, and so on. One day we will get close to 8.00 a.m. This is what it means to press on to perfection.

Today the Lord invites each of us saying, "Come to Me, all who are weary and heavy laden (either because you are married to the old man or because you are married to the Law). Take My yoke upon you (Be married to Me, and let us do everything together)." (*Matthew 11:28–30*).

But that's not all.

The best part of the good news is that when we do work together with the Lord, he does 99% of the works and asks us to do only 1%.

Consider some examples from the gospel of John.

In the first miracle that Jesus did at the wedding at Cana, when the wine ran out, Jesus did not suggest that all the wedding guests should spend the rest of the time in fasting and prayer. No. That would have been what many a Pharisee would have suggested. Many believers have the idea that Jesus is forever taking the joy out of people's lives. But just see what He did at Cana (*John 2*).

We read in *John 2:6* that the six water pots together could hold about 150 gallons (or nearly 700 litres) of water. Now 700 litres is equal to about 3000 glasses. So even if there were about 300 guests at that wedding, this meant that Jesus made 10 extra glasses of wine for everyone there!! He certainly helped all the wedding guests to enjoy themselves. And He is the same yesterday, today and forever.

But notice how Jesus did the miracle. He could have made the wine from nothing. But that would not have been a work done in partnership with others, but a work done by Him alone. So He asked the servants to fill the water pots with water. And then He turned it into wine. He made the servants do the easy part (the 1% part), and then did the difficult part (the 99% part) Himself.

Again, when Jesus wanted to feed the 5000, he could have created the bread from nothing (*John 6*). But then he would have done it alone. So He told the little boy to give Him what he had – 5 loaves and 2 fish. Then the Lord fed the multitude. The boy did 1% and Jesus did 99%.

That boy might have gone home and told his mother that Jesus and he fed 10,000 people. He may even have reversed the order and said that "He and Jesus" fed 10,000 people! (That is how most believers are. Any time the Lord uses them somewhere, they cannot avoid advertising to others what THEY did for the Lord – the souls that THEY won to the Lord, as a result of THEIR preaching and witnessing).

When Jesus healed the blind man (*John 9*), again He asked the blind man to do the easy part – to go and wash his face in the pool of Siloam. Jesus did the difficult part of opening his blind eyes.

When Jesus raised Lazarus from the dead, He told those around to do the easy part again – to roll away the stone. He then did the difficult part of raising Lazarus from the dead (*John 11*).

When the Lord came to His disciples who had toiled all night and caught no fish, He could have filled their boat with fish without their doing anything. But He didn't do it that way. He told them to do something (the easy part) – to cast their net into the sea. He then filled their net with fish (*John 21*).

The great secret of a happy marriage is "doing things together". That is certainly true of our marriage with Christ. When we are married to Christ, we can always do everything together, because He is always with us. We cant do everything together with our marriage partners, because the husband has to go away from the home to work each day. But with the Lord, there is no such problem. We can do everything together with Him all the time.

Who will not want to be married to such a wonderful husband!!

This is true Christianity, and this is the true gospel.

Are you willing then to put off the old man? Are you also willing to die to living by the Law? Are you willing to be married to Jesus alone.

You cannot remain single.

If you are an unbeliever you are married to the old man and one day you will be married to the devil for all eternity.

Or you could be a "believer", but living in a spiritual harlotry – committing adultery with the old man, yielding to your lusts and loving the world (See *James 4:4*).

Or you may be a believer married to the Law. One evidence of this could be your judging others by your own petty standards of right and wrong. Your life may be consisting of various rules and regulations such as "Do not handle. Do not taste. Do not touch" (*Colossians 2:21*), etc. And you criticize others because they do not follow these rules that you have made. You are in bondage yourself and you bring others into that bondage too.

Put off the old man and get rid of your legalistic religion.

Get married to Jesus and do everything together with Him.
Let the truth set you free today.

"If the Law began with such great glory, shall we not expect far greater glory when the Holy Spirit gives us life?" (2 Corinthians 3:7, 8 - TLB)

7

How God Exposes Pharisees in the Church

"Jesus looked at them angrily, for He was deeply disturbed by their indifference to human need." (Mark 3:5 - TLB).

This incident occurred when Jesus entered a synagogue once, and saw a man with a withered hand, and then saw the synagogue-leaders waiting to criticise Him if He healed the man.

Jesus was never angry when people spat on His face or called Him names such as, 'insane', 'Samaritan', 'Satan' etc. But He was angry when people were indifferent and hardhearted towards human need, and when they hindered others from being healed of their 'witheredness'.

We are commanded to "be angry without sinning" (*Ephesians 4:26*). To be angry without sinning is to be angry about the things that Jesus was angry about when He was on earth. All other anger is sin. We must never be angry at the way others treat us or our families. But we must be angry at the way Pharisees treat others in the church in an evil way.

"You should defend those who cannot help themselves. Yes, speak up for the poor and helpless, and see that they get justice." (Proverbs 31:8, 9).

To be angry when people are hardhearted towards other poor, helpless people – that is Christ-like. But to be angry when people are hardhearted towards you or your family – that is demonic. We must distinguish clearly between Christ-like anger and Satanic anger.

The religion of the Pharisees consisted mainly in going to many meetings in the synagogue, and in praying and singing and preaching at the top of their voices, and perhaps in clapping loudly and waving their hands etc., etc., – in order to impress men (*Matthew 6:5, 6*). There are multitudes of Christians like that today too. But our spirituality is never measured by the decibel-level of our singing or of our praying in public. It is measured rather by the depth of our devotion to God and the intensity of our concern for the needs of those around us.

The divine nature is LOVE. The more we have of unconditional love, the more we have of true godliness. There are many people all around us who are withered (weak) in some way or the other in their lives. And Jesus observes our attitude towards them and tests us through them.

God uses the sufferings of godly people to expose the wickedness of those who judge them.

Once when Jesus' disciples saw a man who had been born blind, they asked Jesus whether the man's blindness was the result of his own sin or of the sin of his parents. Jesus replied that it was neither (*John 9:2, 3*). The disciples had been influenced by the teaching of the Pharisees that sickness is the result of sin in a man or in his parents. Jesus is always angry with people who make such judgments on others.

The Pharisees in the synagogue must have felt similarly about the man with the withered hand. They must have felt that they themselves did not have withered hands because they were "holy", and because they had fasted and prayed and tithed! That other man was probably sick because he had not paid his tithes regularly! Or perhaps it was his parents who had sinned.

Children are not Punished for their Father's Sins

It is a very common misconception among many that God punishes children for the sins of their parents. Many believers too hold this heathen idea. And they think they have Scriptural backing for their belief. "For," say they, "does not the Lord say that He visits the iniquity of the fathers on the third and fourth generation" (*Exodus 20:5; Deuteronomy 5:9*).

Yes, the Lord does say that. But if you read carefully, you will notice that the Lord says that He will punish only the children of those who HATE HIM – not the children of sincere believers who slip up and fail.

But that statement of God's was misquoted by the legalists in Israel. They used it as a hammer to beat others with, and to condemn them. And so, 1000 years after God had spoken those words on Mount Sinai, He had to correct its wrong interpretation through the prophet Ezekiel.

He says in *Ezekiel 18:2*: "Why do people use this proverb: 'The children are punished for their fathers' sins?'".

God went on to correct the wrong impression that people had, and told them, "The son shall not be punished for his father's sins, nor the father for his son's. The righteous person will be rewarded for his own goodness and the wicked person for his wickedness." (*Ezekiel 18:20*).

That was clear. But the legalists continued to flourish in Israel and to influence the thinking of the people to such an extent, that when Jesus came to earth, 500 years later, His disciples, even after spending so much time with Him and absorbing His teachings, yet asked Him whether that blind man was suffering for the sins of his parents!!

Pharisaism does not die easily!! We are born with a tendency to judge others and to put the worst construction on their misfortunes.

Job's Sufferings Tested His Friends

Look at the story of Job. Why did God's "anger burn against" Job's three preacher-friends, Eliphaz, Bildad and Zophar (*Job 42:7*). Because they were not right in what they had said about God.

Yet, if you read through the book of Job, you will find that there was not one thing factually wrong, in all that they had said about God, in their sermons to Job. Everything was accurate.

On the other hand, if you read what Job replied to them in his bitterness and self-pity, you will find that Job accuses God about many things. Only occasionally did he speak words of faith. Most of what he said about God was utterly wrong and evil.

Yet at the end of it all, God says that Job had said the right thing about Him, and the three preachers had said the wrong things.

Where were these preachers wrong?

They were wrong because they had judged Job by saying that the loss of his property, children and health was God's judgment on him for some secret sin in his life. Their so-called "discernment" was totally wrong. They had judged a man of God unrighteously by external appearances; and God's anger burned against them to such an extent that He asked them to go and ask Job (the man they had wronged) to pray for them, if they were to be forgiven.

Have you ever done what those three preachers did? If so, be sure that God's anger burns against you too. The safest way is never to judge others. The secret things belong to God. Leave them for Him to judge.

And why did God ignore and overlook Job's many evil words?

First of all, because God saw the uprightness of Job's heart, and recognised that many of Job's hard statements were the result of the pressure he was facing due to his sickness and sorrow. They were not what Job really meant in his heart. Yet what Job said was wrong.

But God could finally forgive and ignore Job's words on a righteous basis, because of one reason: As soon as Job realised his folly, he "RETRACTED his words" immediately (*Job 42:6*). And they were immediately blotted out from God's presence, so that what was left on the record now were only the good words that he had uttered.

Such is the power of God's forgiveness and justification to blot out a man's past record. The good news of the gospel is that we can retract and take back the wrong words that we have spoken against God and men, and they will be blotted out from the record of our lives. But we must do it now, while we are still alive – before we die. The more upright we are, the more quick we will be to do it.

In the record of Job's words, all one can read now are words like:

"The Lord gave me everything I had, and they were His to take away. Blessed be the Name of the Lord... Shall we receive only pleasant things from the hand of God and never anything unpleasant... Even if he kills me, I will trust in Him... I know that my Redeemer lives... He knows every detail of what is happening to me... I am nothing. I lay my hand upon my mouth in silence... I loathe myself and repent in dust and ashes (*Job 1:21; 2:10; 13:15; 19:25; 23:10; 40:4; 42:6* - TLB).

These are all good words. And these are all that the record contains.

But you may say that Job said a lot of other words too. They may be in the book of Job in the Bible. But God says, "Show it to me in My record of Job's life in heaven". And you look – and you can't find even one of the evil words that Job spoke, written there. They have all been blotted out. Such is the result of true repentance and cleansing.

How good God is, and how marvellous is the way He justifies us.

Have you spoken words against God? Confess them to God and ask Him for His forgiveness now. He will justify you immediately.

Have you spoken evil words to men – even accidentally, or under pressure? Confess them to the people concerned immediately, and ask them for their forgiveness. You cannot be justified if you don't ask men for their forgiveness. It doesn't matter whether they forgive you or not. If they don't forgive you, their lack of mercy will bring the merciless judgment of God on their heads on the final day (*James 2:13*). But you would have cleared your record by asking for their forgiveness.

If you have sought to make peace with some Pharisee, and he doesn't want to make peace with you, your responsibility is over. You don't have to grovel at his door forever trying to get him to forgive you. No. Leave him alone, and let God deal with him. You can forget about him.

We all know that Job was sanctified through the sufferings that he went through. That was the main purpose of all his sufferings. But there was a by-product too: God used the sufferings of righteous Job to reveal the wickedness of the religious people who visited him.

They accused Job without knowing the truth – just like many people accuse righteous people today. Most accusations that people make are based on hearsay, and rarely on the basis of first-hand knowledge.

Jesus NEVER judged anyone on the basis of hearsay (what His ears heard). But He was even more radical: He never judged anyone on the basis of firsthand knowledge either (what His eyes saw) (*Isaiah 11:3*). There are very, very few believers in the whole world who are as radical as Jesus was, in this matter.

Pharisees Watch others Closely to Judge Them

In *Mark 3:2*, it says that when Jesus entered the synagogue that day, His enemies "watched Him closely". Pharisees are always like that – they watch the lives of other believers very, very closely in order to find some fault or the other in them.

They watch what the sisters are wearing, to see if their sarees conform to the "simple standard" that believers are expected to live by. They watch to see if there are any ornaments on their bodies or any lipstick on their faces. They watch other believers to see if there is a TV set in their houses, or any other mark of worldliness. They watch the children of others to find some fault in them. Even if they say nothing, they judge with opinions in their minds. They listen carefully to what believers say, in order to catch them in some wrong word.

And the more angry you are with, or jealous you are of another believer, the more closely you are likely to watch his life, to find some fault in him. There may indeed be some trivial fault in his life, or in his wife's saree, or in his home, or in his family. But God will use it to expose the wickedness of your own heart.

God uses the weaknesses and failures of godly people to expose the wickedness of those who judge them.

The Lord says, "Among my people are wicked men who lurk for victims like a hunter hiding in a blind. They set their traps to catch men. Their homes are full of evil plots... Should I sit back and act as though nothing is going on?" (*Jeremiah 5:26, 29* - TLB).

The Pharisees, "plied Jesus with a host of questions, trying to trap Him into saying something for which they could have Him arrested" (*Luke 11:54* - TLB). On another occasion, "they sent other religious leaders to talk with Him and try and trap Him" (*Mark 12:13* - TLB).

The descendants of those Pharisees "who watch others closely" are found in abundance in Christendom today. Let us be "wise as serpents", as we move in their midst, "as lambs among wolves" (*Matthew 10:16*).

One of the quickest ways to become a first-class Pharisee is by starting "to watch other believers closely".

If you want to avoid being a Pharisee, finish once and for all with watching others closely – for that is never done with a good motive, to help them, but always with a view to judge them.

We cannot however, get rid of Pharisaism merely by eliminating from our lives those few characteristics of Pharisaism that we hear others speak of in the meetings, or that we read of in HIDDEN TREASURES. No. The list is endless. Unless we allow the Holy Spirit to deal with us radically, we will never be free. We can eliminate one symptom of Pharisaism from our lives, and still have the disease itself within us.

Have you ever had the experience (even once) of the Holy Spirit showing you some aspect of Pharisaism in your own life, that you had never heard of from another brother's ministry?

If not, I would say that you are not walking the new and living way. You are living by the tree of knowledge of good and evil – good and evil revealed to you by another. Some brother has got light on himself and he shares that in the meeting and you get light. No doubt, you are upright and you get rid of that one thing that was spoken of. But you are living by a second-hand knowledge of good and evil – and that always brings death. You need to learn to live by the tree of life (the Holy Spirit).

The Wounded Man was a Test to the Passers-By

Mercy is a very important antidote to Pharisaism.

Being merciful to others means more than just forgiving those who harm us or do evil to us. It means doing good to others in need.

In the parable of the good Samaritan, Jesus explained what "mercy" meant (*Luke 10:25–42* – see the use of the word "mercy" in *verse 37*).

There we read of a Bible-scholar who questioned Jesus on how to inherit eternal life. Jesus replied that it was by loving God wholeheartedly and by loving one's neighbour as oneself. But the Bible-scholar (like many Bible-scholars today), "wanting to justify his lack of love for some kinds of people" (*verse 29* - TLB), asked Jesus whom the word 'neighbour' referred to. His self-justification identified him straight-away as a Pharisee, and Jesus replied to his question with an illustration.

In the parable, we read first of all of a priest (an elder in God's house) ignoring the beaten man on the roadside. He saw human need there and was indifferent to it. Perhaps he felt the man was being chastened by God for some secret sin in his life. Or perhaps he found fault with the man for walking down that road without any company late at night. He was exactly like the three preachers who preached to Job. How quick we are, when we see people suffer to attribute that suffering to all types of wrongs that we imagine that they must have done, instead of helping them. How indifferent we are to human need! "I was hungry and you never gave Me anything to eat," the Lord says to us, "I was thirsty and you gave Me nothing to drink. I was naked and you never clothed Me. I was sick and you never visited Me. You just sang songs to Me and preached sermons to Me, but never helped me in My need."

> That priest was more interested in getting to the meeting in Jerusalem on time, than in helping a suffering human-being. Remember that a lot of people who are on time for all the meetings finally go to Hell.

After that, a Levite (a brother in God's house), also passed by and he too was tested by God. And he failed the test too. He also wanted to get to the meeting on time, and was indifferent to human need.

These two religious men wanted to get to the meeting to hear God speak to them. Little did they realise that God had already spoken to them on their way to the meeting – and that they had turned a deaf ear to Him. They never heard God tell them that their songs and their prayers and their religion were all worthless, because they were indifferent to the sufferings of a needy man whom they had encountered on the way.

God uses the sufferings of godly people to test the hearts of those who see them suffer.

None of us can throw a stone at these two religious men, for at some time or the other, we have all behaved like them. If we do see ourselves in the Levite and the priest in the parable, then let us repent, and seek to be radically different in the coming days.

We need to recognise that, like the priest and the Levite, we too have been placed on this earth by God, to represent Him. And we have to repent of the fact that we have not represented Him aright.

Finally it was a despised Samaritan (a brother, who belonged to another denomination, that did not have such a pure doctrine as the priest and the Levite had) whom God used to help that beaten man.

That Samaritan was not an elder or a preacher. He was just one of those quiet people who go about doing good to others, looking for opportunities to help those in need, without anyone ever knowing about it. He did not judge that beaten man. He realised that that calamity could have happened to him too. And so he was merciful. He denied himself and spent his time and his money to help a brother in need.

There we see what the new and living way through the flesh really is: Christ manifest in the flesh is LOVE manifest in the flesh. It is MERCY manifest in the flesh. It is GOODNESS manifest in the flesh.

The Prodigal Son's Failure Tested His Elder Brother

In the story of the prodigal son, we see yet another example of an elder brother who is completely indifferent to his brother's need (*Luke 15:11–32*). All that he does is judge his backslidden, younger brother.

If you are an elder in a church, and a brother in your fellowship has backslidden or fallen away, you need to ask yourself why you were so insensitive as to not know about his slipping down, until he actually fell away. Why did you discover his backsliding only after it had become public knowledge to everyone else in the church? How is it you never warned him earlier? It is you who need to repent of your insensitive and hard heart first. And the reason for your insensitivity could be that you yourself are occupied most of the time with your own interests and your family's interests and the good opinions that others in your church and that your elder brothers elsewhere have of you. As a result, you have had no time to think of the needs of your flock.

And when that brother has fallen away and reached the level of the pigs, what do you say then? Do you say, "I knew that would happen. I told him when he left the church that it would go badly with him and that he would end up with the pigs. See what has happened now". You gloat over the fact that that backslidden brother is in a terrible condition, and that you yourself have been proved right!!

There is far more Pharisaism in our flesh than we realise. We are most of the time, far more interested in being proved right than in helping others. Jesus never came to earth to be proved right. He came to seek and to save those who were lost. Do we see how unlike Him we are?

Do you see how Satanic your spirit is – far different from the father-heart of God – when you delight in seeing a brother among the pigs The father was not delighted when his son was among the pigs. He wept. That is how God feels towards backsliders. And every true father in the church will grieve like that. But, as in Paul's time, even today, the church has countless teachers, but not many fathers (*1 Corinthians 4:15*).

Little do you realise that God has used your brother's backsliding to reveal the evil condition of your own heart. It is you whom God is testing when your brother backslides.

"Behold I am against such shepherds", says the Lord (*Ezekiel 34:10*).

The same applies to a husband/wife who is insensitive to the spiritual, physical and emotional needs of his/her wife/husband.

Lazarus' Condition Tested the Rich Man

Why did the rich man (at whose gate the poor beggar Lazarus sat), go to hell? Because he was indifferent to human need. The fire he faced in hell was the fire of the wrath of God – the same fire of God's wrath that burned against Eliphaz, Bildad and Zophar and that burned against the Pharisees in the synagogue when Jesus went there (*Luke 16:19–31*).

The rich man may have judged poor Lazarus, saying that there must have been some secret sin in Lazarus' life for him to be so destitute and helpless in life. He must have felt that he himself had been blessed with material wealth and good health only because God had found him faithful. Little did he realise that Lazarus' condition was a test for him. He kept on deluding himself until one day he woke up in hell. What a shock he must have got then when he saw himself in hell along with the bishops who had deceived him in the temple and the synagogues, with a false religion that consisted only of rituals without Divine love. His shock must have been even greater when he saw that the man whom he had despised all his life – Lazarus – was actually seated in paradise.

But he was not the only rich man who has thought like that. There are many rich believers today who think exactly like that. They think their money, their health and their large pay etc., are all indications of God's blessing on them, and they are indifferent to the needs of others around them who are suffering. Little do they realise that God is testing them through other godly believers around them who are suffering.

There are many, many surprises that religious Pharisees are going to get when they get into eternity.

The more we have understood of God's truth, the greater the danger there is of our becoming Pharisees. Those of us who have had the privilege of hearing the purest and most Scriptural doctrine that anyone is preaching in this country today, are most in danger of becoming super-Pharisees above all the other Pharisees in other denominations.

God uses the sufferings of godly people to expose the wickedness of those who are indifferent to their suffering.

The Woman Caught in Adultery Tested Her Accusers

When the Pharisees brought the woman caught in adultery to Jesus to be stoned, God used that woman's sin to expose the wickedness of the hearts of those Pharisees (*John 8:1–12*).

God uses even the sins of fallen sinners to expose the wickedness of those who accuse them.

If we don't hear the word of Jesus speaking to our hearts constantly saying, "Judge not. He who is without sin, let him cast the first stone", we will end up with that crowd of Pharisees finally, and be eternally cast away from Jesus' presence.

Remember that Jesus was never against sinners. He was only against Pharisees.

8

Faith, Brokenness and Victory

"Our struggle is not against flesh and blood, but against the rulers, against the powers, against the world forces of this darkness, against the spiritual forces of wickedness in the heavenly places" (Ephesians 6:12).

Every believer who is spiritually alive will find himself in the midst of a struggle with evil spirit forces. Those who are spiritually dead however will not sense this struggle, for they are like dead soldiers lying on the battlefield, whom the enemy ignores. Those who struggle with flesh and blood are also ignored by Satan, for he leaves them alone to quarrel and fight with human beings. It is only those who are wholehearted and on fire for the Lord, who are a threat to Satan, and who can fight the battles of the Lord.

Ephesians 6:18, 19 urges us to be on the alert always and to pray with perseverance for all believers, especially for those who faithfully preach God's Word, since they are the prime targets of the enemy's wrath.

An Old Testament Example

In *2 Chronicles 20*, we see a picture of how we can wage this warfare against Satan. There we read of a great multitude that came against King Jehoshaphat. But Jehoshaphat did the right thing, when confronted by so many enemies. He got the whole nation of Judah to seek God in fasting and prayer. Then he prayed to God acknowledging their weakness, their foolishness and their faith.

He said, "O our God, wilt Thou not judge them? For we are powerless before this great multitude who are coming against us; nor do we know what to do, but our eyes are on Thee" (*verse 12*).

This is the secret of all effective prayer – to recognise our weakness and our foolishness, and to trust God utterly to fight the battle for us.

The Weakness of God's Elect

Jesus pictured "the elect" (the church) as a poor, helpless, old widow who has to fight against a strong enemy, with no human help or resources (*Luke 18:1–7*). It is only when we recognise our weakness like that, that we can depend on the Lord. Only then can we exercise faith.

God curses those who lean on human resources with barrenness. He has said, "Cursed is the man who trusts in mankind and makes flesh his strength,for he will be like a barren bush in the desert" (*Jeremiah 17:5*).

Many are constantly defeated by sin, and overcome by Satan, only because they are strong in themselves. They have strong opinions about everyone and everything, they speak stinging words, and they are quick to judge others. God leaves such believers alone, and they never ever become overcomers.

Those who argue and dispute are certainly not weak and powerless. They are strong, and are therefore easy targets for Satan – for he always wins the battle with those who argue. That is how he won the battle with Eve in Eden. Don't ever get into an argument therefore with your husband or your wife or with anyone else – for you will never win. It is always the Devil who will win.

Those who take revenge on others also prove thereby that they are strong people capable of handling their problems themselves. The weak widow needs to plead with the judge (*Luke 18:2*), but strong people don't!!

Others are strong because their bank-accounts are large, or because their employers can be trusted to pay them faithfully on the first of every month. Their trust is not in God, but in man. And so they are barren.

It is only when we come to the end of our own resources that God works mightily to help us. Jesus waited until Lazarus had died – that is, when he had lost all his strength – before He came to help him. He waits on high even today, for us to come to the same zero-point.

Jehoshaphat confessed that he did not know what to do – and that is a good confession to make, for God has promised to give wisdom to all those who acknowledge their lack of it. But we have to ask for wisdom in faith (*James 1:5, 6*). And that was what Jehoshaphat did. He did not merely acknowledge his impotence and his lack of wisdom, He concluded his prayer with an expression of absolute trust in God. He said, "But our eyes are on Thee". In other words, he was telling God, "We are expecting you to work on our behalf". AND GOD DID!!

Three Categories of Believers

There are three categories of 'believers' in the world:

1. Those who have confidence in themselves. Such believers can be identified by the fact that they pray very little or not at all. And they usually never ever fast and pray. Although they don't say so in as many words, by their prayerlessness they testify that they can handle every situation. Such believers can never do an eternal work for God.
2. Those who have no confidence in themselves and who have no confidence in God. They confess that they have no strength or wisdom. But they do not believe that God will work on their behalf. Such believers are usually prayerless too. Even if they do pray, their prayers are invariably without faith. Such can never do an eternal work for God either.
3. Those who have no confidence in themselves, BUT who have total confidence in God. They are aware of their lack of strength and wisdom, but they also believe that God will help them mightily, and do a work in them and through them. Such believers alone are truly spiritual, and only such can do an eternal work for God.

It is good for us to recognise that those in Category 2 above are just as useless to God as those in Category 1. Those in Category 2 may look more broken, but they are not – for unbelief can never be found alongside genuine Christ-like humility. Without faith it is impossible to please God, no matter how broken we may appear to be. Merely acknowledging our inability will not solve our problems. We must trust God too.

To confess that we are rotten, good for nothing, useless and foolish, is not humility, but unbelief!! If we keep on confessing that, we will remain useless forever. False humility like that is often mistaken for the genuine thing by undiscerning believers!

But Jesus told us to learn humility from Him (*Matthew 11:29*). And where do we find Jesus ever confessing that He was useless and good for nothing? Never.

True humility is taking the place of entire nothingness before God, so that God might be all in all. This is the place that Jesus took as a man. This is what we must do too. In that lowly place, we can trust God to do a mighty work in us and through us, and to crush Satan under our feet.

The Battle is the Lord's

As soon as Jehoshaphat finished praying, God immediately sent him a reply saying, "Do not fear, for THE BATTLE IS NOT YOURS BUT GOD'S. You need not fight in this battle. Stand and see the salvation of the Lord on your behalf" (*verses 15, 17*).

To whom does God speak similar words today?

Only to those in Category 3, that we considered above. Pray in faith and speak words of faith, and you will find God working deliverances for you all the time. Those who trust in the Lord will find that they are never ever disappointed or put to shame (*Romans 9:33*). But those who confess only their helplessness will find that they are always put to shame by the enemy.

It is not enough to plough the hard ground (to repent and to be broken). We must also sow seed (the word of faith) in it, if we are to get a crop at harvest time. Those who only keep digging the hard ground without sowing any seed will get nothing. Satan would like either to stop us from digging up the hard ground at all, or to keep us digging forever till the end of our lives!!! Either way, he accomplishes his purposes.

Let us confess that God will crush Satan under our feet (*Romans 16:20*). Satan has no place on our tongues to make us lose our temper or to make us backbite against others. He has no place in our eyes to make us lust after women. No. His place is under our feet – ALWAYS!!

Jehoshaphat worshipped the Lord as soon as he heard those words of the Lord. The next morning he placed "singers and those who praised the Lord in holy attire" in the forefront of the army to lead Judah's soldiers to battle. And as soon as they began to sing and praise the Lord, the Lord defeated their enemies (*verses 21, 22*).

Praising the Lord in Holy Attire

It is the spirit of praise expressing our faith in the Lord that puts the enemy to flight. We see further in that Old Testament passage, that they praised the Lord in holy attire. This is the balance that we need in the church – the spirit of praise and holiness. In Christendom unfortunately, we find believers at two extremes in this matter.

On the one hand we find those who are not living holy lives, who praise God with loud voices and with a lot of emotion. They praise the Lord in other tongues in the meetings and then go home and shout at their wives in their mother tongues!! This is one extreme of deception. To the soulish person who has no discernment, such noise and emotions can look heavenly. But those with discernment will recognise that "all who are in the flesh cannot please God" (*Romans 8:8*), no matter how emotionally they sing in 'tongues', or how loudly they praise the Lord.

At the other extreme, we see many who sincerely judge themselves and seek to live godly lives, but who never seem to have a spirit of praise in their lives. They seem to believe only in exhorting one another all the time – and they look so serious and gloomy while they are at it!

It is written about Jesus in *Hebrews 2:12* that He does two things in the midst of the church:

1. Proclaim the Father's Name.
2. Sing the Father's praise.

Jesus is not only the Messenger of the Father Who brings His Word to us, but also the Praise-leader and the Song-leader in the church.

These then are the two areas in which we must all follow Jesus as our Forerunner and Elder Brother, in the meetings of the church.

When we stand up to share the Word in the church it is the Name of our Father that we must proclaim, and not our own. We are not to stand up to show others how well we can preach, or how faithful we have been during the past week. Neither are we to hit people on their heads with some word that we have found in the Scriptures for their need!! All such preaching is earthly, soulish and demonic, and is a shameful disgrace to the Lord's Name. The testimony of Jesus alone is the spirit of all anointed prophecy (*Revelation 19:10*).

We must also follow Jesus in raising our voices to praise the Father in the church. It is not enough to pray. We must praise God too. Ten lepers prayed to Jesus for healing. Only one praised Him. The proportion unfortunately is about the same in the church today.

A Thorough Victory

The result of Jehoshaphat's approach to the battle was that "not one (of the enemies) escaped" (*verse 24*). What that means for us is that if we approach the battle against Satan in the same way – with faith and praise – not a single one of our problems will remain unsolved. *2 Chronicles 20* begins with "a multitude of enemies (problems)", but ends with "not one enemy (problem) left". God is mightily able to resolve every single problem in our lives.

The people of Judah became rich from the spoils of battle (*verse 25*). And this is the way of acquiring spiritual wealth for us too.

We read further that "the dread of God was on all the kingdoms of the lands when they heard that the LORD had fought against the enemies of Israel. So the kingdom of Jehoshaphat was at peace, for his God gave him rest on all sides" (*2 Chronicles 20:29, 30*). There remains a similar rest for the people of God today too, over all the power of the enemy.

Enduring Until the End in Praise

The sad thing is that Jehoshaphat forgot what he learnt that day, and backslid and compromised towards the end of his life.

We read in *2 Chronicles 20:35* that Jehoshaphat "acted wickedly" and allied himself with idolatrous Israel once again – this time with Ahab's wicked son Ahaziah. Note that the Holy Spirit says Jehoshaphat acted wickedly and not foolishly. The first time

Jehoshaphat compromised, he was foolish. The second time he was wicked. "Like a dog that returns to its vomit, is a fool who repeats his folly" (*Proverbs 26:11*).

Many who once learnt to "praise the Lord in holy attire", don't seem to be able to endure until the end in the same steadfastness. Somewhere along the line they compromise once again. But it need not be like that for us. God is mightily able to help us to endure until the very end.

Praising the Lord in Faith

We praise the Lord at all times and for everything, not because "it could have been worse" (as the psychologists tell their patients to say), but because "it could not have been better" – for God makes everything work for our very best (*Romans 8:28*). That is the praise of faith.

We can all look back at our past lives and see how God made many things that we thought would be bad for us, turn out for our very best. The Lord will do the same in the future too. If we believe that, we will praise the Lord at all times.

In *Psalm 106:12*, we read, "THEN they believed His words; they sang His praise". We read there that the Israelites who left Egypt could praise God only AFTER they saw all their enemies buried under the Red Sea (*verse 11*). That is to live by sight – to praise God after He has solved all our problems. But that was all that was possible under the old covenant, because they could not live by faith.

But now under the new covenant, our heads are anointed with the oil of the Holy Spirit, and we praise God "in the presence of our enemies...because the Lord is our Shepherd and leads us beside waters of rest" (*Psalm 23:5, 1, 2*). We can now praise God, even when the Red Sea has not opened up for us, and when the Egyptians are hot on our heels, and when mountains hedge us up on every side. That is praise that springs from a living faith in an Almighty God.

Even in the valley of the shadow of death, we fear no evil, for we believe that not a hair on our heads can be touched by our enemies without their getting permission from our Heavenly Father. Like Jesus, we can say to our enemies, "You can have no authority over us, unless it is given you from above by our Heavenly Father" (*John 19:11*) Therefore we never have any reason to feel sorry for ourselves, or to complain or grumble about our circumstances or about anyone.

God can make even the blunders that we have committed to work for our very best.

God Uses those Who have Failed

Peter could become a compassionate apostle only after he had blundered and fallen into the sin of denying the Lord three times. It was certainly not God's perfect will for Peter to sin like that. But yet we see that God allowed it in order to do a work in Peter. It made him tender and sympathetic towards those who had failed in life.

Jesus never sinned even once, and yet He was infinitely compassionate and merciful towards sinners. But with the rest of Adam's race, that has not been the case. Those who have never fallen into gross sin usually end up being hard and unmerciful and haughty towards sinners.

When we look at the circumstances through which Peter fell into this gross sin, we see that God could have easily prevented him from even facing the temptation to deny the Lord. Yet God chose not to protect him from those moments of temptation.

In *John 18:15–18* we see that John and Peter followed Jesus to the court of the high-priest. Since John knew the high-priest, the doorkeeper let him in. But Peter could not go in. So John came and spoke to the doorkeeper and gained admission for Peter too. That looked like a good thing at that moment. But notice the fact that Peter would not have sinned that night, if John had not got Peter into that courtyard – for it was only inside there that Peter was questioned, and that he denied the Lord three times (See *John 18:17, 25, 27*).

So we could ask the question, "Why did God allow that to happen? Why didn't He prevent Peter from gaining entry into the courtyard?" Was that a mistake on God's part? No. God in His sovereignty permitted John to get Peter inside, so that Peter could get an education through his failure. He could not have become the leader of the apostles and the leading evangelist of the early church without having completed this course in his education.

Satan had his agents ready to tempt Peter, but he had to get God's permission to do that. But Jesus was praying for Peter that his faith would not fail in that moment of utter failure (*Luke 22:31, 32*). And Jesus' prayer was answered. Peter came out of that experience a broken, compassionate man. Never again in his life would he be able to denounce sinners with harshness. Every time he was tempted to do that, he would remember his own failure and tone down his denunciations.

God can make the very worst things that ever happened in your life to work for your very best, if you have faith. During the seven weeks before Pentecost, Peter may have wished many times that John had not gotten permission for him to enter the courtyard that fateful night, so that he would not have denied the Lord. But then he would not have been broken either, and he would have been unfit to preach the gospel to sinners on the day of Pentecost.

We know that Peter still preached against sin, for he writes in his letter about following in Jesus' steps "who did no sin", and of "ceasing from sin" (*1 Peter 2:2, 22; 4:1, 2*). But now he preached with compassion. This was why he was given the privilege to open the door of the gospel to the Jews on the day of Pentecost, and also to the Gentiles in the house of Cornelius. God could have used James or John in either of those instances. But he didn't. He used Peter – the one who had failed miserably – for he could speak with greater compassion to wayward sinners than those others.

David was another one like Peter. Once when he avoided going to the battlefield through laziness, he slipped up badly and fell into sin – a sin that became like a black mark against him for the rest of his life and for centuries thereafter (*2 Samuel 11:1-5*). The Holy Spirit records, "David did what was right in the sight of the Lord, and had not turned aside from anything that He commanded him all the days of his life, except in the case of Uriah the Hittite." (*1 Kings 15:5*).

Yet God used David's failure to break him and to make him write *Psalm 51* – a portion of inspired Scripture that has blessed millions for many centuries, more than any other writing of David's. David could never have written that psalm if he had fallen into a lesser sin. His failure had to be great and deep and known publicly, so that he might be thoroughly humbled and broken. He was a broken man for the rest of his life.

And Jesus calls Himself the Son of David!!

Brokenness Through Failure

I am not saying that we should therefore go and sin, if we are to become apostles and prophets!! No, certainly not. But if you have already failed miserably, you need not feel that there is no hope for you. You can even yet become a faithful servant of God.

God longs to give us grace, so that we might live in triumph at all times. But He can give grace only to the humble. And often He finds that He can humble us only through allowing us to fall into gross sin. That is not the best way. Jesus was humble, without ever falling into sin. But Peter and David and many other men of God have not been able to manage it, as well as Jesus did. But the wonderful thing is that God uses even Peters and Davids who have failed miserably. But only when they weep bitterly in repentance over their failures – not otherwise.

The first-century writer of "The Epistle of Barnabas" says, "When the Lord chose His apostles who were to proclaim His gospel, He chose those who were the greatest sinners of all, so that He might show that He came not to call the righteous but sinners to repentance."

What God did for Peter and David, He will do for you too.

Stop complaining then that it was because Eve gave you the fruit to eat, or that it was because John asked the doorkeeper to let you into the courtyard that you sinned. Take the blame yourself. It was certainly not the will of God that you should sin and fail. But now that you have failed, God can make even that work for His glory and for your good – to make you a broken man, so that you will never again be hard on others for the rest of your life. So praise the Lord. Overcome Satan then by the blood of the Lamb and by the word of your testimony. Speak the word of faith, and be a broken man, like Peter and David, for the rest of your days.

God planned our lives even before we were born. David says, "You saw me before I was born and scheduled each day of my life before I began to breathe. Every day was recorded in your Book. How precious it is, Lord, to realize that you are thinking about me constantly! I can't even count how many times a day your thoughts turn towards me. And when I waken in the morning, you are still thinking of me!" (*Psalm 139:16–18* - TLB).

That means that God has a diary in heaven for you with your name on the cover. That diary records what His plan for your life is – for every single day. Centuries before you were born, He had already written down who you parents were going to be, and which country you would be born into, and the circumstances that He would arrange to bring you to Christ. It is also written in that diary what trials He would take you through in order to give you a spiritual education. And also how He would make your blunders to work for His glory. All you have to do now is to ask God to show you each day what is recorded in that diary for you. Tell Him that you want to do His will on earth as it is done in heaven, since you can never make a better plan for your life than the one that God has already made for you.

Praise the Lord for such a wonderful Father that we have in heaven and for such a wonderful gospel by which Satan is crushed under our feet, and his accusations against us nullified completely.

9

Are You Serving God or Money?

"No servant can serve two masters, for either he will hate the one and love the other. Or else he will hold to one and despise the other. You cannot serve God and Mammon" (Luke 16:13).

Everyone knows that we cannot serve both God and Satan. But very few know that we cannot serve both God and Mammon (money) either.

Notice carefully the four things that Jesus said here:

1. If you really love God, you will hate money.
2. If you are really holding on to God, you will despise money.
3. If you love money, it proves that you hate God.
4. If you hold on to money, it proves that you despise God.

Most so-called "believers" don't realise it, but they actually hate God and despise Him, because they love money and material things so much. One believer may consider himself doctrinally purer than another. But if both of them love money, then they both hate God. The Pharisees had doctrinal purity (*Matthew 23:3a*) and were religious, but they didn't love God.

You cannot have a neutral attitude towards money, just like you cannot have a neutral attitude towards Satan. You have to either love Satan or hate him. In the same way, you have to either love money or hate it. You will either hold on to money or despise it.

God and Mammon are two opposites, like the two poles of a magnet. If you are attracted by one pole, you will be repelled by the other.

How then shall we hate money? Is it by asceticism and strenuous discipline that we are to do so? Do we have to go and live in a monastery or a "Faith Home" to learn how to hate money?

Jesus did not come to make us hermits or monks or pastors!! He Himself lived a normal life in this world, working as a carpenter for many years to earn His living and to support His mother and His younger brothers and sisters. He earned and used money just like everyone else. Yet He hated money and loved His Father.

An illustration will perhaps help us to understand how we are to hate money. Consider a young girl who is deeply in love with a young man and who feels that she cannot live without him. Then one day she meets another young man who is far more handsome and who appeals to her far more than the first man. Once she has been taken up with this new man, she never again wants to see the first man. How did she get rid of her love for that first man? By the expulsive power of a new affection. That is the way for us to be freed from the love of money too. When love for the Lord Jesus fills our hearts, there will be no place for our former love for money in our hearts. When light fills a room, the darkness flees at once.

So we do not preach that you must hate money in order to love God. No. That is a negative message and will only produce Pharisees, who imagine that they hate money and that all other believers love it. We lift up Christ so that people are drawn to love Him with all their hearts. When they love the Lord with all their hearts, they will then automatically hate money. If someone still loves money, that would indicate that he does not love Jesus with all his heart.

It is not enough merely to say that we do not run after money or that we do not long for it. That is a weak and negative state-ment. Our confession must be positive that we actually hate money and despise it. If that is not true in our lives, it is far better to confess our lack, and to seek the Lord for deliverance. We must be ruthlessly honest with ourselves, if we are to be delivered from self-deception at this point.

Does an increase of money excite us? Are we longing to make more and more money? If our answer is "Yes" to either of these questions, then it is clear that we love money and are serving Mammon.

Many believers are so foolish as to imagine that an increase of money is an indication of God's blessing upon their lives. Some believers even wish that God would help them one day to win a lottery!! Lotteries are one of Satan's means to lure people into the worship of Mammon. A man gets a million rupees by buying a one-rupee ticket. And the money he gets is the money of one million others who are disappointed. That is downright evil.

The Bible says,

"Those who want to get rich fall into temptation and a snare and many foolish and harmful desires which plunge men into ruin and destruction." (1 Timothy 6:9).

Lot wanted to get rich and destroyed his family in the process. Balaam wanted to get rich and lost his calling as a prophet and went to hell. Gehazi wanted to get rich and not only missed the opportunity to be a prophet, but also brought leprosy upon himself and his children.

Again and again we have seen tragic examples of believers who were progressing well, but who suddenly backslid, because they wanted to get rich and began to pursue after wealth beyond their needs.

Satan lured such believers at first by giving them a little taste of the enjoyment that wealth could give them (just like drug-pushers give a little taste of drugs to young people). Thus Satan whetted their appetites for Mammon. Little by little he led them on, until they finally "got hooked on Mammon" and plunged themselves and their families into ruin and destruction. Lives that were meant to build the church, are now being wasted in the pursuit of money. Such believers have sold their birthright for a bowl of porridge! Think what regret will be theirs in eternity!

All sensible believers will therefore never pursue after wealth, just like they won't jump off from the 10ᵗʰ floor of a building. They know that either of these actions will destroy them. They realise that they can't ignore the warnings of Scripture and still expect God to protect them.

One doesn't have to actually run after money to fall away. One can love money in one's heart and still fall away, for "the love of money is a root of all sorts of evil, and some by longing for it, have wandered away from the faith, and pierced themselves with many a pang" (*1 Timothy 6:10*). Just as a young man can love a girl in his heart without actually running after her, even so, one can love money secretly in one's heart, without actually running after it. That is enough to make a believer fall away.

No-one can build the church who does not determine to love Jesus with all of his heart. We will know that we love the Lord with our whole hearts, when we begin to hate and despise money.

How many are willing to make this the test of their love for the Lord? All our boasted "spirituality" is worth ABSOLUTELY NOTHING, if we still love money.

Jesus spoke of two aspects of our responsibility in relation to money when He said: "Render to Caesar the things that are Caesar's and to God the things that are God's." (*Matthew 22:21*).

1. Giving Caesar what belongs to him refers to being RIGHT-EOUS in money matters.
2. Giving God what belongs to Him refers to being FAITHFUL in the use of money.

Being Righteous in Money Matters

We cannot hate and despise money, if we don't FIRST go through the kindergarten class of being righteous in money matters. This means that we must give to Caesar what belongs to Him. In other words, we must not have anything with us that belongs to someone else.

We should not be owing anything to the government (Caesar), by having cheated it of taxes that are due to it. Neither should we have in our possession anything that was borrowed from someone and not returned, or that was taken from someone (or some office) by cheating, or any money that was not righteously earned. There is a curse on anything that we have that is unright-eously earned. If you are in debt to someone, it is better to starve and to pay back your debts than to have a curse hanging over your head and your children's heads.

We must also return all money and things that we have taken wrongfully in the past – even if it takes many years to complete such restitution. Zaccheus's home was blessed the moment he decided to make restitution (*Luke 19:9*). Your home will be blessed too, the day you make such a decision. Even if your debt is very large, don't get discouraged. Start paying back whatever you can – even if it be only Rs. 10 a month. The Bible says that where there is a willing heart, God will accept you, according to your ability to repay, and not according to whether you have actually repaid everything or not (*2 Corinthians 8:12*).

It is no use hanging a plaque in your house that says, "GOD BLESS OUR HOME", if you have things and money in your home that have been obtained unrighteously. God can never bless such a home.

If you don't settle all such financial irregularities in your life, you will drag a chain behind you wherever you go. If the Lord were to return suddenly, you would be found unworthy to be raptured. Many so-called "believers" will be left behind in the rapture just for this one reason.

The Bible commands us to "owe nothing to anyone" (*Romans 13:8*). That means we should avoid all borrowing and all buying of things on credit.

It is better to "Save now and buy later", than to "Buy now and pay later" as the world tells us to do.

If in an emergency, you do borrow money from someone, then make sure you pay it back at the earliest opportunity. Sell the gold in your house if necessary in order to pay it back. If you promise to return borrowed money by a certain date and are unable to do so, go to your creditor, humble yourself, ask for his forgiveness and request him to give you an extension of time to return the money. It is unrighteous to keep quiet about the matter, and return the money whenever you feel like it.

In cases where you don't know where your creditor is now, the money can be given to the church – for all money belongs to the Lord ultimately (See *Numbers 5:8*). But we must never keep such money ourselves, for there is a curse on all money that we have that is not lawfully ours.

The slavery of believers to Mammon is seen most clearly at weddings. There we see covetousness and greed displayed unashamedly. Consider the giving of a dowry that is practised by so-called "believers" from every single denomination. Those who ask for dowry are a disgrace to the name of Christ and are certainly not His disciples. Those who expect to get a dowry from the bride's parents are no better.

Consider also the great waste of money there is at many wedding receptions. There is nothing wrong in having a good wedding reception if you can afford it. Jesus Himself made extra wine for people at a wedding reception. But many believers borrow money in order to have such a grand reception. That is evil. It is far better to have a simple reception, than to borrow money and have a grand one. But alas, the thought in the minds of many at such times, is What will others say?", and not "What will God say?". They fear man's opinion more than they fear God's.

We must never adulterate this message in the church at any cost. It is far better to build a small church with a few whole-hearted people in our locality, than to build a large one with many compromisers.

Being Faithful with Money

Once we have learnt to be righteous in money matters, we must move on to being faithful with money.

What did Jesus mean when He said that we were to give to God what was due to God? Did He mean that we were to give Him our tithes (10% of our income). Under the old covenant, that was all that the Israelites had to give to God. That was God's due. Once they had done that, the rest was their own. But under the new covenant it is different.

Jesus demonstrated by His own life that we are to give 100% to God. Jesus said to His Father, "ALL THINGS that are Mine are Thine" (*John 17:10*). He came to deliver us from the bondage of the Law (the bondage of tithing) and to bring us into the glorious freedom of grace (the freedom that comes from giving 100% to God cheerfully).

We give everything to God, not because of some commandment to do so, but first of all, because we recognise that everything is lawfully His in any case. "The earth is the Lord's and all it contains (whether houses or lands, or gold or silver or whatever)" (*1 Corinthians 10:26*).

If we have earned much, we should not forget that "it is the Lord Who gives us power to make wealth" (*Deuteronomy 8:18*). So our money is not our own for us to use as we like. We cannot spend, or lend, or give our money to anyone, without asking the Lord for specific directions in each case – because all our wealth is His now.

Secondly, we give the Lord everything, because we love Him with all our hearts. Our money is now held in a joint-account with our heavenly Bridegroom. We don't keep a separate account for ourselves, and give Him 10% every month!! No. We say,

"LORD, ALL THAT IS MINE IS THINE". Only such a man can say that he loves God and hates Mammon.

To be faithful with money means therefore that we love the Lord so much that we spend the minimum necessary on ourselves – on food, clothes, and in decorating our houses, etc.

This is the meaning of "forsaking all our own possessions" (*Luke 14:33*). Even if we have many earthly things, we do not possess any of them any more as our own. We are detached from all material things. Thus we are delivered from worshipping Mammon in our lives.

A pure heart is one that has forsaken all earthly possessions. A pure heart is different from a clean conscience. A pure heart is one that has place in it ONLY for God, and no place for Mammon or anything else.

It is through money and through earthly things that God tests a man to see if He can commit spiritual responsibility to him or not.

Jesus said,

"If you have not been faithful in the use of unrighteous mammon, who will entrust the true riches to you" (Luke 16:13).

God can never use any man in His service whom He has not first tested with Mammon. The reason why many churches lack the prophetic word today, is because their leaders have failed the Mammon-test.

The reason why most preachers and believers never get any fresh revelation from God, year after year, is because they are not faithful in the way they use their money. They are lavish in the way they spend on themselves – on their food, clothing and houses, and even on tourism and sightseeing etc., etc.

Faithfulness with Mammon implies avoiding all wastage. After feeding the 5000, Jesus said to His disciples, "Gather up the fragments that nothing may be lost" (*John 6:12*). Jesus hates wastage of every sort. That applies not only to loaves and fishes, but also to time and money.

Godliness involves being frugal in expenditure and being careful not to waste anything that God has given us.

If we are not faithful in the use of money, then the only understanding we will ever get of God and His Word will be second-hand – from the preaching of others who are faithful.

And such second-hand revelation is NOT revelation at all, but only dry knowledge. It may be accurate knowledge, but it will lack the anointing of the Holy Spirit. This is the condition of the vast majority of believers today – in all groups.

Full-Time Christian Workers and Money

Let us now consider the case of "full-time Christian workers".

> Notice first of all (in the gospel-records), that the Lord never once called an unemployed person to be His apostle. Peter, Andrew, James, John and Matthew (whose 'calls' alone are described in the Gospels) were all working at their earthly occupations when the Lord called them. They left their profitable earthly jobs, when the Lord called them to follow Him.

There are three reasons why the Lord called only those who were working in a secular profession:

1. We have to prove our faithfulness in handling money in the secular world before God can give us a spiritual ministry. And we can prove our faithfulness with money only when we have earned that money ourselves. Money that we have received as a gift, can easily be given to others or to the Lord's work because we don't feel the pinch ourselves. Such giving doesn't prove our generosity at all, because it is someone else's hard-earned money that we are giving away!! It is when we learn to give money that we have worked hard to earn ourselves that we can prove our generosity.

2. God governs the world on the principle of sacrifice – as we see from Calvary's cross. So there must always be a sacrifice in our going out to serve the Lord. Otherwise we cannot be servants of the Lord. If we gain financially by our going out to serve the Lord, or if we earn more than those we serve, or if we live at a higher standard than those we serve, through the offerings that they give us, then our so-called "godliness" has become a means of profit for us and not loss and sacrifice. Then we are like the money-changers in the temple whom Jesus drove out. Jesus will drive us out too.

3. The people to whom we minister God's Word in the church are all working in secular professions. If we ourselves have had no

experience in the struggles and difficulties that there are in a secular job, we will only be able to preach theories to our flock, and not practical truths that work in the secular world. We have to preach from our experience, not from our knowledge.

For these three reasons, Jesus chose apostles only from those who were already faithfully doing their secular jobs. He has not changed His mind in the 20th century. He chooses only such people to serve Him even today.

Most "full-time Christian workers" in India however have never done an honest day's work in any secular occupation in their entire lives. Most of them went to Bible-school because they did not get admission into any other college, or because they were unemployed. And now many of them have amassed such wealth through their Western contacts, that they have been able to buy houses and lands, that they could never have bought if they had worked in secular jobs!! Their version of 'Christianity' has brought them astounding financial profits!! But the Bible calls them "men of depraved mind, without the truth of God" (*1 Timothy 6:5*).

The biggest hindrance to the testimony of Christ in India today is such men who give the impression to our countrymen that Christianity is a Western religion, promoted by Western money and Western preachers.

Western preachers give their agents in India large sums of money, or free trips to the West and thus hinder God's work. The believers in India become so dependent on their Western leaders for spiritual help, that apostles and prophets never arise in India, and the churches here never learn to stand on their own feet either spiritually or financially.

The time has come in India for "full-time workers" to begin serving the Lord like the apostle Paul did – who made tents to earn his living – (*Acts 18:3; 20:33–35*). We too must learn to support ourselves, and not be dependent on other believers and churches for our living, in this day.

It is true that "the Lord has directed those who proclaim the gospel to get their living from the gospel" (*1 Corinthians 9:14*). But many "full-time workers" have misused that verse to justify their indiscriminate receiving of money from others, and have ended up serving Mammon, and not God.

Paul goes on to tell us in the next four verses (*1 Corinthians 9:15–18*), how he considered it a privilege and an honour to support himself, while serving as an apostle of Christ. The Holy Spirit led Paul to serve the Lord like that, so as to expose the false preachers in his day – "to cut out the ground from under the feet of those who boasted that they were doing God's work in the same way" as Paul was (*2 Corinthians 11:12* - TLB).

The Holy Spirit has led ALL the elders in all of our churches in India too in the same way: We support ourselves, and preach the gospel and shepherd the flock, without receiving any offerings from those to whom we preach. Thus we expose those preachers who serve Mammon in India today. This has caused many money-loving preachers to be angry with us, just like such people were angry with Jesus and Paul in their time.

Anyone who has joined us, and sought for financial gain from the flock for his service, has been ruthlessly exposed by the Lord and removed from our midst – even as the Lord exposed Judas Iscariot and Demas. (Thankfully however, this has happened only once in the last 20 years.)

There are many who claim to be "apostles" in India today. But how many among them are serving the Lord as Paul did? None that I know of!

Many preachers may read our books and listen to our tapes, and preach our messages as their own. BUT THEY WILL NOT IMITATE US (IN THE WAY WE SUPPORT OURSELVES AND PREACH THE GOSPEL FREE OF CHARGE), BECAUSE THEY WORSHIP AND SERVE MAMMON.

Therefore they have no direct revelation from God of the truths of Scripture. They get their messages second-hand from our books and tapes. This lack of Divine revelation is the clearest proof that they are unfaithful in their dealings with money and material things.

Peter and John told the lame man in the temple that they had no silver or gold to give him (*Acts 3:6*). Even though the believers in those days gave so much of their money to these apostles (*Acts 4:35*), the apostles knew that such money was given for distribution to the poor. So nothing stuck to their hands, even when so much money passed through their hands. Those apostles refused to receive any payment for their services! Thus, through being faithful with money, they retained the anointing of God upon their lives until the end, unlike many in these days, who started well, but who have ended up like Judas Iscariot.

The New Testament warns us of the ERROR of Balaam, the WAY of Balaam and the DOCTRINE of Balaam (*Jude 11*; *2 Peter 2:15*; *Revelation 2:14*).

The example of Balaam who loved money and collected money from the rich, for his preaching, has been highlighted again and again in the New Testament, to warn us against falling into such a pitfall ourselves.

Godliness must never become a means of gain to any of us – either in terms of money, honour, profitable business-contacts or any other type of material gain. Genuine godliness will actually bring us loss of honour and money. Thus we pay a price for what we believe.

Jesus lost both wealth and honour when He came to this earth. And if we follow Him, we will lose wealth and honour too. It is only people like Judas Iscariot who will make a profit through their spiritual contacts. If your version of "godliness" has brought you honour, wealth or financial profit,then you must be following Judas, and not Jesus.

The real gain that godliness brings will always be spiritual.

God is looking in our land for a generation of radical men and women who desire to please Him alone, and WHO WILL DEMONSTRATE TO THIS WORLD THAT ITS ENTIRE VALUE-SYSTEM IS TOTALLY WRONG AND THAT ALL THAT IS EARTHLY IS WORTHLESS UNLESS IT IS USED TO SERVE THE LAW OF LOVE.

Such people will show forth by the way they live, that money is not everything, education is not everything, comfortable living is not everything, worldly honour is not everything, etc., etc. Instead they will stand upright for the truth in an upside-down world, and show forth to the world that: GOD ALONE IS EVERYTHING. Will you be one such person?

May the Lord raise up many such men and women in our land today.

10

Standing in the Gap Before the Lord

The Lord says,

"I searched for a man among them who should build up the wall and STAND IN THE GAP BEFORE ME for the land, that I should not destroy it; but I found none." (Ezekiel 22:30).

God tells Ezekiel in this chapter why the Israelites had gone into captivity to Babylon (*verse 15*). Jerusalem had become a city of murder, where "slanderous men were shedding blood" (*verses 3, 9*).

Today we find that many churches have also come into a similar state. Compare the sins listed in *Ezekiel 22* with those we find among many today. Believers slay their fellow-believers – with their tongues (*verse 6*). Many Christian groups claim that they alone constitute the true church, and condemn other believers who don't agree with them. Many believers disrespect their parents and their spiritual fathers (*verse 10*). We can say that churches with such believers have indeed become cities of murder. And so they, like Israel, have gone into captivity, and failed to be effective witnesses for Christ in their localities.

In Israel, we read that God searched for one man who would stand before Him and pray for the land (*verse 30*). But He found none. About eight centuries earlier, when Israel had sinned, Moses had stood in the gap. And so God did not destroy the Israelites. But now there was no-one to pray. All sought their own. If they prayed at all, they prayed only for themselves and for their families. And so they went into captivity.

The Man God Finally Found

However, seventy years later, God finally did find a man to stand in the gap – Daniel. God had promised through Jeremiah that seventy years after the Israelites were taken to Babylon, they would return to Jerusalem (*Jeremiah 25:12, 13*). When Daniel was over 87 years old (having lived through the whole period of the captivity), he read that prophecy of Jeremiah.

Daniel was the wisest of all men who had lived up until his time – even wiser than Solomon. [We can see this from the fact that when God wanted to point out the cleverness of Satan, He compared Satan's wisdom with Daniel's, and not Solomon's – and Daniel was a young man living in Babylon when God said that (*Ezekiel 28:3, 14*).]

But when Daniel read what God had promised, He didn't use his clever mind and conclude that God's Word would be fulfilled automatically, without his having to do anything. No. (That type of attitude is fatalism, not Christianity). He mourned and FASTED and prayed earnestly that God's Word would be fulfilled (*Daniel 9:2, 3*). And that was how God's Word was fulfilled. There we see how the wisest man who ever lived, did not lean on his own wisdom or sense of logic, when reading God's Word and praying.

God does not work apart from a man standing in the gap and praying.

Daniel was also a righteous man. When God wanted to point out the three most righteous men that ever lived, He mentioned the names of Noah, Daniel and Job – and Daniel was a young man, when God said that!! (*Ezekiel 14:14, 20*). Just as Joseph had kept himself pure in Egypt, Daniel had also kept himself pure in Babylon (*Daniel 1:8*). Yet this righteous Daniel when he knelt before God, acknowledges himself as a sinner!! (*Daniel 9:4–11*).

One mark of a genuine man of God, is that he is more aware of his own sins than anyone else's. Like Paul, all true men of God consider themselves to be the chief of all the sinners in the world. The sins that disturb their consciences are not the dirty ones that common sinners fall into. No. Their consciences are so sensitive that they consider even prayerlessness as a sin (*1 Samuel 12:23*). They are also quick to identify themselves with the sins of the people with whom God has placed them. It is only the prayers of such righteous men that are effective with God (*James 5:16*).

It was Daniel's prayers that moved men (and even kings!) at that time to rebuild God's temple, and the city of Jerusalem itself finally – as we read in the books of Haggai, Zechariah, Ezra and Nehemiah.

Daniel himself was too old by then to go and work in Jerusalem. But God had young men like Zerubbabel, Zechariah and Joshua to do that. But these man needed the prayer-backing of Daniel to accomplish their task – just as in an earlier time, Joshua and his men needed the prayer-backing of Moses to overcome the Amalekites (*Exodus 17:8–13*).

Freedom from Selfishness

God is looking for men and women even today in our land, who will stand in the gap for the church – selfless people, who are not taken up with just their own needs, but who are concerned about God's work.

Many believers think that sanctification means just the refinement of their personal conduct and behaviour. But true sanctification makes a person selfless like God – or in other words, like Jesus.

No-one knew what God was like until Jesus came to earth, and explained Him (*John 1:18*). And what do we learn of the nature of God, when we look at Jesus? We see that the Divine nature is one that is willing to give up everything, and to be inconvenienced to any extent, if as a result, sinners can be saved from their sin and brought back to God.

> Jesus did not come down from heaven because He wanted to gain something for Himself. No. He came to earth totally for the benefit of others. He lived for others. He fasted and prayed and gave Himself – all so that others might partake of God's salvation. It is this spirit that is so rare to find even among the leaders in the church today. Although many speak of partaking of God's nature, very few actually partake of this selfless love for others.

Many are willing to deny themselves and take up the cross if that will bring them some benefit – perhaps some spiritual benefit such as a place in the Bride of Christ, but still something for themselves. But if we were to ask ourselves, what we have denied ourselves purely for the benefit of others, we may discover that the answer is, 'Almost nothing'.

There are many in our midst who despise full-time Christian workers, feeling that such people don't have the fullest light. But before you criticise them, it may be good to ask yourself whether YOU would be willing to resign your job in order to preach the gospel to the heathen. It is easy to despise others who don't have as much light as we have. But despite all the light that we have received, we may still be loving our comforts and unwilling to give up anything costly for the Lord.

Jesus gave up His place in heaven in order to come and live on this earth for 33½ years, without any of the comforts of modern civilization – only so that others might hear the gospel and be saved. He also resigned His job as a carpenter, so that He might devote all His time to be a 'full-time worker' to preach the gospel to others.

It is this Spirit of Christ that has urged missionaries through the years, to suffer hardship and loss, so as to take the gospel to heathen lands, where the Name of Jesus had never been heard, to bring others to Christ. Those on the other hand, who travel and stay in 5-star comfort these days, and preach the gospel, are all tourists, by comparison.

It is good for us to read the biographies of saintly missionaries who gave up everything for the Lord, so that we too can be challenged by their sacrifice and their devotion to the Lord. A holiness that does not lead to a sacrificial life is a deception – for true holiness is not just being free from sin, but being free from Self-love too.

The fire of God does not fall on many today, because they have not placed everything on the altar. They are willing to give up everything for the Lord, except their jobs and their comforts. If anything on this earth is still valuable and precious to you, then you are not a disciple of Jesus.

Inward and Outward Sacrifices

It is true that many in Christendom have placed a greater emphasis on the external sacrifices, than on the inner sacrifice of taking up the cross, that the New Testament calls us to. But it is possible for us, in an over-reaction to that error, to go to the other extreme of living a life where all our sacrifices are only inward – and sometimes imaginary!!.

If Jesus had made only inward sacrifices, He would never have left heaven and come to this earth. And if His apostles had made only inward sacrifices, the gospel would have never gone further than Jerusalem!! Jesus and the apostles were balanced, and knew that God wanted them to make inward as well as outward sacrifices for the gospel's sake.

It is only those who are willing, like Jesus and the apostles, to go through hardship and inconvenience in order to bless others, who will be able to carry the burdens of others in prayer and to stand in the gap in prayer in the church today.

It is a great deception to imagine that we are walking in the footsteps of Jesus, or that we are sanctified and spiritual, if we are occupied only with our own needs and hardly ever take time to pray for others.

> Jesus lived in such a way that others might be blessed and brought near to God. This is the new and living way that He has inaugurated for us.

That which we give priority to in our lives is invariably a clear indication of what we really worship. If, for example, we never forget to eat or sleep or go to work, every single day of the year, but find ourselves having forgotten to pray on many days, then food and sleep and money must certainly have become our gods.

How much of our time and energy and money are we willing to sacrifice for the Lord? We may find a false comfort in the fact that under the new covenant, we are not commanded to set apart one day in the week and 10% of our income for the Lord. Many who used to give 10% of their income to God when they were in the denominations, have now backslidden to the point where they give God almost nothing at all. This is certainly not the way that Jesus walked. Such a state of affairs has come about, because comfort and prosperity have become their gods.

Perhaps we don't lose our temper or lust after women now. That's good. But these can never be a substitute for the external sacrifices that should also be found in our lives, if we are to follow the Lord.

Many of us have now come to the place where we are able to explain the doctrine of 'victory over sin' better than the apostles themselves!! But we need to get a little more light on the utter selfishness that characterises our way of life. Spiritual instability is often caused by the fact that a person's 'knowledge' leg is over 3 feet long while his 'life' leg is only about 1 or 2 inches long!! And he still spends his time seeking to stretch his 'knowledge'-leg!!! Despite the purest revelation of God's truth that he may have, his selfishness still remains uncrucified.

Men with a Burden and a Concern

The whole movement of Israel FROM BABYLON TO JERUSALEM was born and carried forward by men who were selflessly concerned for the furtherance of God's work. For this they fasted and prayed.

This is how it is going to be in the church in our day too. Those who seek the honour of God's Name, the coming of His kingdom and the fulfilment of His will on earth as it is in heaven, will fast and pray and bind the workings of evil spirits, and thus accomplish God's purposes.

Daniel was a man who frequently fasted and prayed.

Ezra too was a man who knew how to fast and pray when leading a group of Israelites from Babylon to Jerusalem (*Ezra 8:21*).

Nehemiah wept and fasted and prayed when he heard that Jerusalem was broken down and its walls burnt with fire (*Nehemiah 1:4*). He didn't criticise the Israelites in Jerusalem for being lazy or selfish. No. He fasted and prayed for them. He was so burdened that even his boss (the king) noticed his grief. Finally, Nehemiah gave up his position and his comfort in the palace in order to go and rebuild the walls of Jerusalem.

> Have we ever been grieved like Nehemiah, because the work of the Lord is not progressing? Have we ever fasted and prayed like he did, because we saw that things were not going well in the church? Do we ever pray for those who preach God's Word to us?

I wonder if we realise that those who serve God and preach His Word faithfully (and their families) are targets of Satan's wrath. They are high on Satan's hit-list. Let me recommend that you stop criticising them, for Satan can do that job quite well, without your help! Instead pray for them a little more in the coming days, that they will be preserved from the attacks of the enemy.

As in Israel 2000 years ago, so in India today, many of the Lord's sheep are scattered here and there, without shepherds to care for them. Many are the hirelings in our land who work for pay. Few are the shepherds who are willing to lay down their lives for the flock. No-one has the right to preach God's Word to God's flock if he has no burden for the sheep, and if he does not pray for them regularly.

Pray that the Lord of the harvest will thrust forth shepherds after His own heart into the harvest at this time (*Matthew 9:36–38; Jeremiah 3:15*).

Fasting and Prayer

Fasting is not popular among this generation of believers.

But Jesus said that once He (the Bridegroom) left the earth, His disciples WOULD fast. He did not say that His disciples might fast. No. What He said was that "in those days MY DISCIPLES WILL FAST" (*Luke 5:35*). All who fast and pray are not necessarily disciples of Jesus. But all who ARE true disciples of Jesus will certainly fast.

It was when the apostles were fasting and worshipping the Lord, that the Holy Spirit spoke to them to send Paul and Barnabas out to preach to the Gentiles. Thus began the first great missionary movement of the early church into Gentile lands (*Acts 13:2, 3*). Paul and Barnabas went out and established churches, and then fasted and prayed again before handing those churches over to local elders (*Acts 14:23*).

Even husbands and wives are exhorted by the Holy Spirit to fast from a sexual relationship at times for the purpose of prayer (*1 Corinthians 7:5*).

God told Israel that Sodom was their sister, because, like Sodom, they were proud, lazy and selfish, and fond of good food (*Ezekiel 16:49*). From this we see that the sexual sins (that Sodom became famous for) were closely related to their gluttony and their love for fine, tasty foods. There is a very close connection between lack of self-control in the sexual area and a life characterised by laziness and overeating.

Don't let God call Sodom your sister too.

Binding the Workings of Satanic Powers

At one time when Daniel had finished a season of 21 days of prayer and partial fasting, God revealed to him that through his prayers the evil spirit ruling over Persia had been overcome (*Daniel 10:2, 3, 13*).

In a similar way, in our day, the hold that evil spirit-forces had over Communist lands for nearly 75 years, was broken, because God's people in many parts of the world had fasted and prayed and wrestled against them. As a result, these lands have now been opened up for the gospel.

Jesus said that certain categories of demons could be cast out only through fasting and prayer (*Matthew 17:21* - KJV).

We who are living in India now have a great responsibility to fast and pray and wrestle against the evil spirit-rulers that have such a strong hold over many believers and unbelievers in our land. There is so much of compromise in Christianity in India; and there is no country in the world that has as many heathen temples, or whose people are more in bondage to idolatry, than India. We have all seen during the past few months especially, how these evil religious spirits have stirred up millions of our countrymen to such unbelievable violence and religious frenzy.

Now is the time for God's people in India to stand together and bind the workings of these Satanic forces. If God can find a remnant in our land who are free from prejudices and grudges, and from laziness and selfishness, and who are determined never to fight against human beings, but only with evil principalities and powers, then the evil spirits that influence India's millions will begin to tremble.

Our calling as a church is to enforce the victory that Christ won on Calvary's cross, over all the forces of Satan hovering over India.

God is looking for men and women in the church today who will stand in the gap and pray – who will fast and pray – and bind the workings of these evil religious spirits that have blinded and led astray so many in our land, for so many years. Thus the Name of the Lord Jesus Christ will be glorified and honoured in India.

You don't have to feel guilty, if you don't feel burdened to pray like this, for God does not give the same burdens to all His people. But if you are burdened that there should be A PURE TESTIMONY for the Name of the Lord Jesus in India, then let us stand together in fasting and prayer in these days, so that God's purpose will be fulfilled.

If your heart responds to this call, then begin by praying every day that the workings of these evil spirit-rulers in India will be bound and restrained. Then proceed to fasting and prayer. And then pray with others who have a similar burden. And if you want your prayers to be answered, be careful at all times to keep yourself pure, and free from the sins of judging others around you and being a busybody in their matters. Preserve yourself at all costs as a sharp instrument for God, and don't allow your effectiveness to be neutralised by any kind of sin.

11

Two Types of Backsliders and
Two Types of Leaders

There are two types of backsliders – and Jesus spoke about both of them in *Luke 15*. The first one He described as a lost sheep. The second one He pictured as a lost son.

The Lost Sheep

"What man among you, if he has a hundred sheep and has lost one of them, does not leave the ninety-nine in the open pasture, and go after the one which is lost, until he finds it ... There will be more joy in heaven over one sinner who repents, than over ninety-nine righteous persons who need no repentance" (Luke 15:4, 7).

It was not a goat that the shepherd went seeking. It was a sheep – a sheep that had once been in the fold. This parable refers to a born-again believer who has backslidden. But he has not left the church in a spirit of rebellion. Like a sheep, he went astray through carelessness. Perhaps he was deceived. Perhaps, because of his weakness, he was overpowered by attractions that proved to be too much for him. The Good Shepherd goes after such a sheep UNTIL He finds it. We who are under-shepherds must do the same. We must go after those who have backslidden from the church through carelessness, Satanic deception and their lusts.

One of the charges that the Lord made against the shepherds of Israel, 600 years before the birth of Christ was this:

"The sheep that are sickly you have not strengthened, the diseased you have not healed, the broken you have not bound up, the scattered you have not brought back, nor have you sought for the lost ... and they were scattered for lack of a shepherd, and they became food for every beast of the field and

were scattered. My flock wandered through all the mountains and on every high hill, and My flock was scattered over all the surface of the earth; and there was no-one to search or seek for them... Behold I am against these shepherds... Behold I Myself will search for My sheep and seek them out... I will deliver them from all the places to which they were scattered on a cloudy and gloomy day" (Ezekiel 34:1–12).

Many sheep are lost on a cloudy and gloomy day – a day when they are discouraged and depressed by the pressure of some trial or sorrow that proves to be too much for them. The Lord says that He will seek for such sheep and bring them back. He seeks for them through "shepherds after His own heart" (*Jeremiah 3:15*). It must be the longing of all of us in the church – both brothers and sisters – to be shepherds after God's own heart, who can seek out the many lost sheep around us today.

There are many who are ready to criticise and condemn such sheep saying that they should not have wandered so close to the edge of the cliff, or that they should have stayed in the midst of the flock and not wandered off by themselves seeking other pastures, or that they should not have listened to the voices of the false shepherds, etc., etc. There is no dearth of specialists who are ready to give an accurate analysis of the reasons for the backsliding of these sheep. What is sadly lacking is shepherds after God's own heart who will go after these lost sheep and bring them back to the fold. This is the great need in the church today.

The Lord's True Flock

The Lord describes His flock in this parable as "righteous persons WHO NEED NO REPENTANCE" (*Luke 15:7*).

Amazing words! Is it possible that there are human beings on earth who are living in such victory over ALL conscious sin in their lives, that the Lord Himself certifies that they need NO repentance?

Yes there are such godly ones even today on earth. They are the Lord's true flock. No church in the world consists entirely of such people, for every single group in Christendom has been corrupted by infiltrators and outsiders, who have been sent by

Satan to corrupt the witness of the church. Even Jesus had a Judas Iscariot in his "church". The apostles had their Ananiases and Sapphiras and Demases too. But none of these people ever got power in the church in those days. That is how Jesus and the apostles preserved the purity of their fellowships.

These righteous persons whom the Lord described as not needing any repentance, are the real church of Jesus Christ. They don't need any repentance, because they are judging themselves all the time. They keep short accounts with God, striving always to have a conscience that is without offense towards God and towards men. They are quick to confess the slightest sinful thought or attitude to God, and equally quick to confess the slightest sinful word or deed to men as well. Thus they live each day of their lives as those who need no repentance – because they are living in constant repentance. These and these alone constitute the Lord's true flock.

Every church that the Lord is building today should have a core of such "righteous persons who need no repentance", if it is to be a pure and powerful testimony for the Lord in these last days. Every backslider (lost sheep) must seek to join and fellowship with such a flock of godly people, and not with any group that calls itself a 'church'.

It is no use engaging in evangelism and bringing in a lost sheep to a fold that consists of ninety-nine sheep who are riddled with diseases and who are biting and tearing each other apart – sheep who are not righteous and who have plenty to repent about themselves! A lost sheep will be far more lost if it were to join such a fellowship! Such a sheep would be far safer out in the wilderness than inside such backslidden churches. To bring lost sheep into some churches these days is like admitting sick people to a dirty hospital where they acquire sicknesses that they never had when they came to the hospital!!! What is needed first of all, before engaging in evangelism, is a thorough cleansing within the church itself.

The Lost Son

"A certain man had two sons... The younger son gathered everything together and went on a journey into a distant country, and there he squandered his estate with loose living... When he came to his senses, he said, 'I will get up and go to my father, and will say to him, "Father, I have sinned against heaven, and in your sight; I am no longer worthy to be called your son; make me as one of your hired men.""" (*Luke 15:11–24*)

This backslider is different. He was a son who sought his own, and rebelled against his father and went away, criticising his father and his home and his family-members. He criticises the elders and the brothers and sisters in the church, and seeks to exalt himself at their expense.

In this parable, unlike the earlier one, we do NOT see God going after the lost son. He allows the lost son to reap what he has sown and to suffer the consequences of his rebellion. And when the son has come to an end of himself, he comes back to his father's house on his own. He is not carried home on anyone's shoulder. He repents and comes back on his own, sick and tired of himself. God's love for such backsliders is manifested in NOT going after them, but allowing them to reap what they have sown until they have come to an end of themselves, and then to return to Him in brokenness and genuine repentance.

Since most believers in every church are carnal, they lack wisdom, and so do not know how to distinguish between these two types of backsliders. On the one hand, they seek to carry rebellious sons on their shoulders back into the church, and criticise the elders for not doing this. On the other hand, they ignore the lost sheep and do nothing to go after them and bring them back. They console those who should be rebuked, and they rebuke those who should be comforted.

To feed rebellious sons and daughters (who have left their Heavenly Father and His house) is the best way to ensure that they never ever return to God. Such acts are not acts of compassion but acts of folly. It is because many seek their own honour and reputation, that they speak kind words to rebellious believers, instead of rebuking them. Their words and actions only ensure that these lost sons stay out in the far country even longer - and in some cases forever. The blood of these prodigal sons who perish in the far country and go to hell, will finally be on the hands of those who helped and comforted them.

(NOTE: A word of caution is necessary for all Pharisees at this point: Just because someone has left YOUR group and joined some other fellowship, does NOT mean that he has left the

Father's house – for the Father's house is much wider than your petty little group! So don't use this parable or the above paragraph to justify your Pharisaical attitude towards someone who has left your group. Perhaps you need to realise your own need that you are like the elder brother in the parable, and not like the father at all).

When these rebellious sons do return to the church in true brokenness and repentance, our hearts must be wide open to welcome them, and we must not allow them to wallow in their misery and sorrow. This is where the difference between those who are like God and those who are like the Pharisees is seen clearly. Although it will take time for confidence to be restored and for these prodigal sons to be restored to any ministry in the church, yet as far as acceptance and fellowship are concerned, this must be IMMEDIATE, warm, and wholehearted – exactly as the Lord described in the parable, with feasting and rejoicing!

Discern Between the Two

The great need in our day is for our love to be guided by wisdom. Paul's prayer was,

"I pray that your love will grow in real discernment, so that you may approve the things that are excellent (as opposed to those things that are merely good)" (Philippians 1:9, 10).

If we are to distinguish between these two types of backsliders around us, we will have to develop the habit of listening to the voice of the Holy Spirit in our spirits at all times, so that we don't live either by Pharisaic rules or by worldly compassion. If we depend on our own reason, we are bound to make mistakes. We need to be humble, and we need to hate our own human strictness and our own human love.

Shepherds and Fathers

There are two types of leaders in the church too. The good ones are like shepherds and fathers. The self-seeking ones are like hirelings and tutors. It is by our attitude towards backsliders that we can discern which category we fit in to.

Just like true shepherds are rare in the church, true fathers are rare too. Just like hirelings abound on every hand, teachers who seek their own, abound too. Why? Because it is easier to be a hireling than to be a shepherd, and it is easier to be a teacher in the church than a father. It costs heart-pain and burden and battling in prayer against the wolves and the roaring adversaries, if we are to be fathers and shepherds. And most people don't want to pay such a price to serve the Lord or to build the church. Most people try to build the church cheaply.

Paul, as a true father to the failing, carnal Corinthian Christians, told them, "I do not want to shame you. Even if you have countless teachers in Christ, yet you do not have many fathers. In Christ Jesus I became your father" (*1 Corinthians 4:14, 15*).

The father (in Jesus' parable) did not put his repentant son on probation for six months. Nor did he make him live in the servant's quarters. No. He believed in him, and had hope for him. "Love believes all things and hopes all things" (*1 Corinthians 13:7*).

A true father will never, never shame his children or reveal their faults to others, even when they backslide. Teachers in schools and colleges however rejoice to make their students' follies known to others. By our attitude towards the faults and failings of others, we can know whether we are fathers or teachers.

The Lord is looking for true fathers and shepherds in the church.

12

A Church Triumphant Over Satan

There were only two occasions when Jesus spoke about the church – in *Matthew 16:18* & *18:17–20*. And on both these occasions He spoke about Satan battling against the church. In the first reference, Jesus spoke of Satan attacking the church directly through the forces of spiritual death – through evil spirits. In the second instance, He spoke of Satan trying to corrupt the church indirectly through a brother whom he deceives and captures, and who unconsciously becomes his agent.

But whichever method Satan adopts, the Lord has given us the authority to bind Satanic workings, and to release those who are captured by him (*Matthew 16:19; 18:18; 2 Timothy 2:26*). We must exercise this authority in the church with all boldness.

The Importance of Divine Revelation

Jesus told Peter here that HIS church was going to be built on the Rock that Peter had just confessed – "the Christ, the Son of the Living God" (*Matthew 16:16*). Peter got that revelation on Jesus from the Father (*verse 17*). We need revelation on Jesus too.

> A knowledge of Christ that comes merely through the study of the Bible, or by hearsay, is not enough. "No-one knows the Son except the Father" (*Matthew 11:27*) – and only the Father can give us that revelation. Only then will we be able to build the church on the same foundation that the apostles built the church in their day.

Only the Father can show us that Jesus Christ is the Son of God, Who has triumphed totally over Satan, and Who now has all authority in heaven and earth, all things being placed in subjection under His feet.

Only the Father can show us that Jesus Christ came in our flesh, was tempted in all points as we are, and yet did not sin,

109

but overcame the world totally, giving us the hope that we too can walk on earth as He walked (*1 John 2:6*).

Any amount of human argument and reasoning can never be a substitute for Divine revelation.

Preserving the Church from Satan's Agents

Jesus said that the church He builds has one identifying mark: It overpowers the gates of hell (the forces of spiritual death). On the other hand, if a church is itself overcome by the forces of spiritual death – that is, by jealousy, or strife, or a competitive-spirit, or by honour-seeking, or immorality, or the love of money, or worldliness, or by bitterness, or pride, or arrogance, or Pharisaism, etc., then we can be certain that that is NOT the church that Jesus is building.

There are carnal believers in every church who are slaves to these sins. But they must forever be kept on the periphery (in the outer court), so that they are given no ministry, or responsibility, or power in the church. None of us should ever be a part of any church that does not seek to battle these evils constantly.

Satan perpetually seeks to destroy the church. And most of the time, he tries to do this by infiltrating into the church through his agents. Jude speaks of "certain people who have crept into the church unnoticed" (*verse 4*). Like the Gibeonites who deceived Joshua (*Joshua 9*), there are many today who have deceived the elders and pretended to be disciples and crept into the midst of the churches unnoticed. But how did these people manage to deceive the elders? Perhaps because the elders were overawed or bribed by their wealth or their worldly position. In all Babylonian denominations, it is the people who have worldly position or wealth who are able to influence the decisions taken in their group, even if they are not elders. But it must never be so in our midst. If we are not careful however, the Gibeonites will come into the church too.

God may sometimes allow these people who have "crept in unnoticed", to be in the church for a period, to give them time to repent and to be converted. At times, He may also allow these infiltrators to fulfil the task that Lucifer fulfilled in the third heaven ages ago. Lucifer dragged away one-third of the angels with him, when he rebelled and fell away (*Revelation 12:4*) – and thus the third heaven was cleansed of all rebellious elements. So today also, the Lord allows self-seeking people to come into the church, so that when they leave, they can take other insincere people along with them, and thus cleanse the church of all rebellious elements! This is part of God's wonderful wisdom.

We can see an example of this, from what the Lord has done again and again in the churches in India. He has wonderfully and deftly arranged circumstances, and exposed and removed from our midst those who sought position in the church, and who had a divisive and a controversial spirit (See *Romans 16:17*). He has caught the clever people and the big people who came into our midst "in their own craftiness" (*1 Corinthians 3:19*) and thus frustrated their secret plans to "hijack" the church!! This is a mark of the Lord's care for us, and of His intense desire that there should be a pure, untainted testimony for His Name in our land.

We praise the Lord that He watches over us constantly to preserve us from such Satanic attacks. "Unless the Lord guards the city, the watchmen keep awake in vain" (*Psalm 127:1*) It is only where brothers dwell together in unity that the Lord can command His blessing (*Psalm 133:1*) – and only a united church can triumph over the gates of Hell. So the Holy Spirit works mightily in our midst, to preserve us in that unity.

Now we must be alert and pray that the Lord will continue to do this work in the future too. His perpetual promise to us is: "I will remove from your midst the proud, exulting ones, ... and I will leave among you a humble, lowly people, who take refuge in the Name of the Lord" (*Zephaniah 3:11, 12*). The church can be built in unity only with humble, lowly people.

It is not our task to drive anyone away from the church with human zeal – for "the anger of man cannot achieve the righteousness of God" (*James 1:20*). No. Our task is to receive all who come to us, and to show them the way of life. But the Lord is jealous to preserve His church in purity, and so He Himself will expose and remove self-seeking people in His own way and in His own time, just like He drove the money-changers out of the temple at the right time.

Jesus spoke in *Matthew 18:17–20* of a brother who sins and thus brings defilement into the church. We must remember that such a brother is usually not aware of the fact that he has become a tool in Satan's hands. Jesus therefore said that we must go and speak to him privately at first, in order to WIN HIM. That is always our aim: To win the brother – to win him away from Satan, and for the Lord and for His church. If he does not listen, we must try to win him again, this time with one or two more brothers. If he still does not listen, then we must tell the church about him. And if he does not listen even to the church, then he must be put out of fellowship, so that he can see his own need and repent, and so that others are not defiled by his spirit.

We must be strong in the Lord to pray and bind these workings of Satan, so that God's work in the churches in India proceeds unhindered. We must also learn to forgive every brother quickly and totally, so that Satan does not get any advantage over our own lives (*2 Corinthians 2:11*).

Knowing Satan's Tactics

If we are to wage effective spiritual warfare, we must not be ignorant of Satan's schemes, devices and tactics.

From the way Satan tempted Jesus with food in the wilderness, we conclude that Satan will seek to tempt us also through the legitimate desires of our bodies. Jesus spoke to His disciples to beware of being concerned too much about food and clothing. If food or fancy clothes have a hold on us, Satan will certainly have power over us, for our kingdom will then be of this world. We have to be careful that we don't train up the young girls in our churches to be taken up with pretty dresses, lest they grow up to be captivated by Satan.

Lucifer became Satan when he (as the head of the angels) began to consider himself as someone important among the angels (*Ezekiel 28:11–18*; *Isaiah 14:12–15*). It is thus that Satan enters the hearts of many believers too. Whenever a brother begins to think that he is somebody important in the church, it is clear that he has been infected by the spirit of Satan. Then he will be ineffective for spiritual warfare, even if undiscerning believers around him feed his ego by making him feel important!!

When a brother speaks for a long time in the meetings, beyond the measure of his spiritual content, and vomits out his Bible-knowledge on the poor long-suffering, brothers and sisters in the church, that is a clear indication that he begun to feel that he is somebody important, and that he is superior to others. That is the spirit of Satan. And yet, we have often found, that such a brother does not even have victory over such an elementary matter as getting offended. If he is exhorted after the meeting to be brief, he gets offended. It is clear that such brothers are not living in a constant self-judgment, for if they were, they would have felt the Spirit convicting them of their pride and their arrogance.

It is such brothers whom the Devil makes his agents. But we have to preserve the church in purity, and so we must keep on exhorting such long-winded brothers to be brief – even if they keep on getting offended with our exhortations. Those who have bitterness and sourness in their spirits should not speak in the church-meetings for more than one minute. And in that one minute let them confess their hope that they will become whole-hearted quickly and get rid of their sinful attitudes.

When Jesus warned His disciples against the use of titles, He was warning them of this very same Satanic spirit that seeks to exalt itself above others in the church. A "Reverend" is greater than an ordinary brother. A "Pastor" is also greater than an ordinary brother. But Jesus said that we were all to be just ordinary brothers. Let the Babylonians keep their titles. Let us avoid them, even in spirit. Always seek to be the junior-most brother in the church, in your spirit, and you will not only be safe yourself, but also effective in your battle against Satan.

Lucifer was also discontent with the circumstances that God had placed him in. That was how he became the Devil. This spirit of discontentment is what Satan is now spreading in people's hearts around the world. And many, many believers have picked up this infection too.

There is nothing wrong in improving your earthly, material circumstances. But when you see another brother having more than you, don't envy him, don't desire what he has, and don't expect any gifts from him. Be content with what it has pleased God to give you. "He who hates gifts will live" (*Proverbs 15:27b - KJV*). Don't be ignorant of Satan's schemes. The moment you are discontent with your salary, your house, the colour of your skin, or any such thing, you open your heart's door to Satan.

We Do Not Struggle Against Flesh and Blood

"Our struggle is not against flesh and blood, but against the rulers, against the powers, against the world forces of this darkness, against the spiritual forces of wickedness in the HEAVENLY PLACES" (Ephesians 6:12).

3500 years ago, Moses came down from Mount Sinai and brought the Israelites a promise from God of a kingdom on this earth. But 2000 years ago, Jesus came down from heaven and brought us the promise of a heavenly kingdom. This is the fundamental difference between the new covenant and the old. If we don't understand this, we will not be able to wage an effective warfare against Satan.

Our kingdom is not of this world. And so we must NEVER, NEVER fight or quarrel with human beings concerning any matter. This is the Number One requirement for effective spiritual warfare. One of the chief ways by which Satan tries to sidetrack believers from their calling, is by getting them to fight or quarrel with others – with their relatives or their neighbours or their brothers and sisters. And invariably the quarrel will be concerning some earthly matter. Thus he succeeds in dragging believers down from their heavenly position to this earth and its affairs, and thus makes them ineffective in their battle against him.

If you want to fight Satan effectively and to build the church, determine that you will never get involved in a dispute with any human being, or concerning any earthly thing. We must not even wage imaginary battles in our minds, with others. We must not have a single complaint against anyone.

And we must not have an inward demand on anyone either. We must not, for example, have a demand that people should treat us with respect, or with consideration, or show love to us, or that they should never cheat us or deceive us etc. We must not have such expectations even from our marriage-partners. All such disputes and complaints and demands are indications that a person's kingdom is of this world, and that he has given place for Satan in his heart. And such people are doomed to live a miserable life.

God is the Only One with whom we have to do (*Hebrews 4:13*). All our circumstances (including the way others treat us) are designed by our loving Father for our very best – to conform us to the likeness of His Son. Therefore we have no room for any complaints against anyone, but plenty of room for praising God at all times.

The Spirit of Praise

In each of the 7 glimpses of heaven given in the book of Revelation, we see the inhabitants of heaven continuously praising God with a loud voice – sometimes as loud as thunders and as the noise of roaring rivers. This is the atmosphere of heaven – one of continual praise, without any complaints or demands. And this is the atmosphere that the Holy Spirit desires to bring into our hearts, our homes and our churches as well. It is thus that Satan will be driven away from all these places.

I read of a fiery brother (who lived in the last century) who used to frequently praise God with loud 'Hallelujahs'. One day, one of the staid, dead Christians around him, who was irritated by this spirit of praise, asked him what the brother would do if God finally sent him to hell. To this the brother replied, "If I go to hell, I will keep on shouting 'Hallelujah' and the praises of God there, until the Devil tells me to get out of Hell, lest I infect others in hell with the spirit of praise!!"

No, there is no place in Hell for those who have a spirit of praise! The ones who go to Hell are those who are full of complaints and demands against others. They were like that when they were on the earth and they carry that evil nature with them when they leave the earth too.

Satan has paralysed the vast majority of Christians, and made them ineffective in spiritual warfare against him, because he has succeeded in getting them infected with the spirit of murmuring and complaining against their brothers and sisters, against their relatives and neighbours, against their circumstances, and even against God Himself.

We overcome Satan, when we obey the following exhortations:

"Let the peace of Christ rule in your hearts to which indeed you were called in ONE BODY; and be thankful" (Colossians 3:15). *"I urge that thanksgivings be made FOR ALL MEN"* (1 Timothy 2:1).

"Always give thanks FOR ALL THINGS in the Name of our Lord Jesus Christ to God, even the Father" (Ephesians 5:20).

We are exhorted first of all to be thankful for all whom God has called into Christ's Body. If the choice had been left to us, we might not have called many of those whom God has called – especially those who belong to some other group than ours!!! But God's wisdom being higher than ours, even as the heavens are higher than the earth, He obviously had a different opinion about them than we have. And if we are wise, we will re-align our thinking in line with God's.

Once we have learnt to be thankful for our brothers and sisters in Christ's Body, we can then learn to give thanks for all men and then for all our circumstances. We know that our Heavenly Father sovereignly controls all men and all circumstances. If we really believe this, we will certainly praise God at all times, and thus prove that our kingdom is of heaven and not of this world. Then Satan will lose his power over us. Only then will we be able to wage an effective warfare against him.

There is a wonderful word written in *Revelation 12:8* that no place was found in heaven for Satan and his demons. This is how it must be in our lives too – in our hearts, in our homes, and in our churches. SATAN AND HIS HOSTS MUST FIND NO PLACE IN ANY OF THESE PLACES.

13

No Man Can Boast in God's Presence

"No man should boast before God…just as it is written, 'Let him who boasts boast in the Lord'" (1 Corinthians 1:29, 31).

God does everything in such a way that no man will ever be able to boast in eternity concerning anything that he himself did or accomplished. God is a jealous God and He will never give His glory to anyone else (*Isaiah 42:8*).

When the rich young ruler had gone away from the Lord, because he was unwilling to give up his riches, Jesus told His disciples that it was as difficult for a rich person to enter God's kingdom as it was for a camel to go through a needle's eye. The disciples then asked the Lord who could then be saved. The Lord's reply was that it was impossible for man to save himself. God alone could save man (Read *Mark 10:24–27*).

A rich person is not just one who has plenty of money. One can be rich in many ways – in talents, in Bible-knowledge, in one's opinion of one's own spirituality and in many other ways.

The kingdom of God is very, very large. But the gate into it is as narrow as a needle's eye. It is impossible for a camel to go through it. But what is impossible for a camel is the easiest thing in the world for an amoeba (the smallest of creatures). It is all a question of size.

It is pride that makes a man rich and hinders him from entering the kingdom of God. And pride is such a subtle, evil thing that it is impossible for man to save himself from it. We may repent of many sins, and even get victory over anger, the lust of the eyes and the love of money and many other sins. But at the bottom of it all, it is still possible to be proud of our salvation and our victory. Deep down in our spirit it is possible to have an attitude that says,

"I thank God that I am not like other men or even like Christians in other denominations." (See *Luke 18:11*).

It is impossible for us to save ourselves from the evil of pride. Only God can save us. We must recognise this and humbly submit to God and ask Him to save us. Or else at the end of our lives, we will discover that despite all our experience of "victory" and of "being in the Body of Christ", we were just first-rate Pharisees.

So we ask with the disciples, "Who then can be saved?" And the Lord answers us as He answered them, "With men it is impossible, but not with God" (*Mark 10:26, 27*).

Salvation as described in the New Testament has three tenses – past, present and future. If we are born again, we have already been saved from the PENALTY of sin. We are now to be saved from the POWER of sin. And one day, when our Lord returns in glory, we will be saved from the very PRESENCE of sin.

And each one of these aspects of salvation is the work of God. God's Word tells us very clearly:

"By grace you have been saved through faith; and that not of yourselves, it is the gift of God; not as a result of works that no one should boast" (Ephesians 2:8, 9).

Jonah was delivered from the fish's belly only when he finally acknowledged that "salvation can come only from the Lord" (*Jonah 2:9*). The next verse states, "THEN the Lord commanded the fish to vomit Jonah out on dry land". God waited until Jonah acknowledged that he could not save himself. And He waits on high until we too acknowledge that we cannot save ourselves from any sin or any difficult situation. Then He commands deliverance for us as He did for Jonah.

When we find ourselves in a "tight" situation, like Jonah was in, instead of complaining and murmuring, if we would only learn to give thanks to the Lord and to confess that salvation comes from the Lord alone, we will find deliverance coming sooner.

Salvation is not a self-improvement program. That can only change us on the outside. The work of God changes us on the inside.

God works in such a way that man can never glory in anything. If we are to experience a thorough salvation from sin, then we must be saved from glorying in anything that the Lord has done for us – including the victory He has given us over sin.

The smaller we are (in our own eyes), the easier it is for us to get "an abundant entrance into God's kingdom" through the needle's eye (*2 Peter 1:11*). And one proof that we are really small in our own eyes will be that we never despise another human being – whatever his religion or his denomination, or his lack of light (on the truths that we have understood) may be. Even when we look at the worst of human beings, we will say to ourselves: "There go I but for the grace of God".

Jesus always referred to himself as "the son of man" – or in other words "an ordinary man". This is what we must recognise ourselves to be too, at all times. If we have been saved from the penalty of sin, it is God's mercy alone that gave us that salvation. If we are now being saved from the power of sin, that too is the result of God's mercy and grace given to us freely. So what do we have to glory in? Nothing.

Consider an illustration: If others were to admire a beautiful painting that you had painted, you could be tempted to be proud of your accomplishment. But when they admire what someone else has painted, how could you even be tempted to be proud. We could use this illustration to the work of salvation that God accomplishes in our lives. If it is we who have improved ourselves or sanctified ourselves, then we could be proud of it. But if it is God Who has done this work in us, then how can we ever be proud of it?

What is the quality of our "sanctification"? Is it merely a work of moral improvement? If so, we have experienced nothing Divine or supernatural in our lives, but only done what any man with a little determination can do. But if it is a genuine work of God that has taken place in our lives, then we have been given eternal life (God's nature) – and that is a free gift from God (*Romans 6:23*). (God's nature cannot be manufactured by us in any case). And if what we have become is the result of God's free gift, then all boasting is ruled out.

So if you are proud of your victory over sin, then you must have manufactured it yourself!! In that case, your victory is useless and certainly not the genuine thing. And the sooner you throw it away, the better. Seek instead to partake of the Divine nature.

Paul said that he did not want to be found having a righteousness that was of his own making, but only with the righteousness that came from God(produced by God) through faith in Christ (*Philippians 3:9*).

In Romans, we see the development of the gospel message chapter by chapter. Here is a brief outline of the first few chapters:

- *Chapters 1 to 3* – The guilt of man made plain.
- *Chapter 4* – Justification (being declared righteous by God) by faith.

- *Chapter 5* – We have freedom of access to God now through Christ's blood.
- *Chapter 6* – Our old man was crucified with Christ, so that we need not sin any more.
- *Chapter 7* – We are free from the Law and from a legalistic attitude towards the Christian life.
- *Chapter 8* – We can now live in the Spirit and put our lusts to death daily.

The result of such a salvation is that "we are more than conquerors in Christ" (*Romans 8:37*). The danger at the end of all this however, is that we can imagine that this work of salvation is OUR OWN accomplishment.

And so we have three wonderful chapters that follow *Romans 8*, that explain that salvation is a work of God, from start to finish. Although these chapters (*Romans 9 to 11*) refer to God's dealings with Israel under the old covenant primarily, the Holy Spirit seeks to apply these truths to our lives today.

Romans 9 – God's Sovereignty

Abraham's two sons Ishmael and Isaac grew up in the same home with the same father. Yet God chose only one of them – Isaac (*Romans 9:7*). That was not because God was partial, but because He is sovereign. He has the absolute right as the Creator of the universe to do exactly what He likes and to choose whomever He likes for any task. No-one can question His right, because He created all things for His pleasure, and as Paul says (at the end of these three glorious chapters), "From Him, through Him and to Him are all things" (*Romans 11:36*).

Isaac had two boys, Esau and Jacob who grew up in the same home with the same parents. Yet God chose only the younger Jacob. "Though the twins were not yet born, and had not done anything good or bad, in order that God's purpose according to His choice might stand, not because of works, but because of Him Who calls, it was said, 'The older will serve the younger'" (*Romans 9:11, 12*). There was nothing unjust in this action of God's, for He is the sovereign Ruler of the universe.

Moses and Pharaoh both lived in Egypt at the same time and in the same palace. Yet God raised up Moses to be a prophet of His. And Pharaoh was raised up, "to demonstrate God's power in him and that God's Name might be proclaimed throughout the whole earth" (*Romans 9:17*), through the hardness of Pharaoh's heart and the judgments that God would send on him as a result.

In all these three examples, we see the sovereignty of God in choosing people. We need to see the same sovereignty at work in our salvation too. Why did God chose you and not some of your relatives – your brother, your sister, your uncle etc.? Was it because you were better than them? Certainly not. Perhaps you were a greater crook and a hypocrite than them (like Jacob was). Yet God chose you. It is sheer mercy and grace.

What shall we say in the light of all this? We can only bow before this Almighty Sovereign God and worship Him with all our hearts, and acknowledge that He alone is worthy, and that our salvation is entirely (100%) due to his grace. It is true that we accepted what He offered us. But the work was entirely His.

There is nothing that so humbles man to the dust as the fact of God's sovereign choice of His children. That is why clever people find it difficult to accept it, and fight against it, and try to twist the Scriptures to make them mean what they don't mean.

It is not because a man determines to be a child of God (or to be holy), or because he decides to run faithfully, that he is saved. It is only because God has shown him His mercy. It is God Who "grants us repentance unto life" and it is He Who "works in us to desire His will and to do His will" (*Acts 11:18; Philippians 2:13*). What can we glory in then?

Here is what *Romans 9:16* says: "It does not depend on the man who wills or the man who runs, but on God Who has mercy".

And here is what *1 Corinthians 4:7* says: "What do you have that you did not receive? If you did receive it, why do you boast as if you had not received it?"

Memorise these two verses and keep them always in your heart. They will help in keeping you small in your own eyes at all times.

The new birth does not come through the will of the flesh (human determination), but by the will of God (Divine determination) (*John 1:13*).

Jesus told his disciples, "You did not choose Me but I chose you" (*John 15:16*). Do we realise that fact?

Very often we imagine that it was WE who had accepted the Lord as our Saviour and that that has made the difference between us and the unbelievers. It is good for us therefore to remember that it was God Who chose us. And He chose us in Christ before we were born – in fact, even before He created the world!! (*Ephesians 1:4*).

From start to finish, our salvation is 100% from God – so that no man might boast in God's presence one day.

Have you done something wonderful for the Lord and for His kingdom? If so, then try your best to forget about it. Recognise that you could have done nothing if God had not given you health, strength, intelligence, gift, talent, opportunity, knowledge of His Word and of Himself etc., etc. The list is endless. How can you glory then?

When we are taken up with how spiritual we have become or how much we have done for the Lord, we are already Pharisees. A true disciple is one who is taken up with the Person of the Lord Himself at all times.

There are many things God does for which he gives us no explanation. There are many prayers for which His answer is "No", and we don't understand the reason why. It is as impossible for God to explain all His dealings to us as it is to fill the Indian Ocean into a cup. God's wisdom is like an ocean. But our minds are only like a little cup.

Scripture says, "Who are you O man to criticise God?" (*Romans 9:19, 20* - TLB). When we are small in our own eyes we don't have any complaints about God's ways. We just submit to God, even when we don't understand His dealings, because we accept His sovereignty.

Romans 10 – God's Righteousness

Israel had great zeal for God (*Romans 10:3*) – but it was zeal without a knowledge of God, for they did not understand that God's righteousness could not be produced by their own efforts. This was essentially where they failed. And this is where many Christians pursuing righteousness also fail today. They want to be holy, but they pursue after it with a human zeal that makes them haughty and arrogant towards others.

> *"Not knowing about God's righteousness, and seeking to establish their own, Israel did not subject themselves to the righteousness of God"* (Romans 10:3).

Our own righteousnesses (our very best works) are all like filthy rags in God's sight (*Isaiah 64:6*). They are an abomination in God's eyes – and that is why they must be thrown away.

It was self-righteousness that made the elder brother (in the story of the prodigal son) into a Pharisee. In the first part of the parable, it is the younger brother who is outside the father's house. But at the end of the story, it is the elder brother who is outside, while the younger brother is clothed and rejoicing inside. Jesus constantly exposed self-righteousness as the worst of all sins – worse even than adultery and murder. Yet very few Christians understand the seriousness of this sin.

It is self-righteousness that makes a Christian look down on other Christians, and that makes preachers preach to others without judging themselves first. Such attitudes are like filthy rags in God's sight.

Is your righteousness something that God has wrought in you, by making you partake of His nature, or is it something that you attained by gritting your teeth, by getting up at 4.30 a.m. every morning, by fasting and prayer and by yogic self-control? Humility is the test.

God is determined that no flesh will be able to glory in His presence in eternity. So the righteousness that you have produced through your own efforts will be worth nothing at all in the final day. You might as well realise it now.

> At the very beginning of our Christian lives, God declares us righteous because of our faith in Christ. Otherwise we would not even be able to stand before Him. And then, God sanctifies us by making us partake of His nature increasingly. It is He Who gives us the grace to be faithful and unyielding in the moments of temptation, so that we do not sin. It is He Who gives us the abilities and the gifts of the Spirit whereby we are able to serve Him and be useful in His vineyard. So we see that salvation from start to finish is from God – 100%.

"God is found by those who did not seek for Him and He manifests Himself to those who did not ask for Him" (*Romans 10:20*). Those are words that most Christians don't even know are found in the New Testament. Paul says there that Isaiah was very bold to make such a statement – and we can be certain that Isaiah was very bold, for that statement goes against the grain of every self-righteous Pharisee of all times.

Humble people however have no problem accepting these facts, for they recognise that their salvation begins and ends in God. Jesus is the Author of their faith (the One Who began it in their lives) and He is the Finisher of their faith too (the One Who will bring it to completion) (*Hebrews 12:2*). So they have nothing to boast about at all.

Romans 11 – God's Faithfulness

To the early Christians it looked as though God had rejected Israel finally, and that the promises that God had made to Abraham had been annulled. But the Holy Spirit says through the apostle Paul, very clearly that "God has not rejected His people whom He foreknew" (*Romans 11:2*).

"If some did not believe, their unbelief did not nullify the faithfulness of God" (*Romans 3:3*).

God is faithful to His promises, and that is why He has brought the seed of Abraham back into the land of Israel in this century, after they had wandered about in many countries for over 25 centuries.

"There is also at the present time a remnant according to God's gracious choice" (*Romans 11:5*). This is because God is faithful to His promises. Even though a hardening has come upon Israel at this time, one day "all Israel will be saved" (*Romans 11:25, 26*).

God is merciful even to those who crucified His Son.

We who are under the new covenant can learn something from that, and find our comfort in the faithfulness of God to His promises. Not one promise that He made to Abraham concerning his seed has failed or will fail. And not one promise that He has made to us His children will ever fail. The faithfulness of God will see us through to the very end of our lives, and until Jesus comes again.

"I am confident of this very thing that He Who began a good work in you will perfect it until the day of Jesus Christ" (Philippians 1:6).

"I know Whom I have believed and I am convinced that He is able to guard what I have entrusted to Him until that day" (2 Timothy 1:12).

Romans 12 – The Only Adequate Response

In view of these attributes of God that we have considered, what shall we do? Shall we take advantage of His goodness and go forth and sin even more. Far be it from us to take advantage of the goodness and mercy of God like that.

Paul says that in view of all the mercies of God that He has showered upon us, the only adequate response that we can make is:

1. To present our bodies as a living sacrifice to God; and
2. To present our minds to be renewed each day to think like Him, instead of like the world.

Thus we will be able to prove and fulfil the perfect will of God for our lives. (*Romans 12:1, 2*).

There are mean, selfish Christians (as there have always been) who can only think of taking advantage of God's goodness and grace, and who therefore take sin lightly, because they know that God is so merciful and forgiving. But any believer with even the slightest sense of gratitude will long that he might never sin again, and that he might live his whole life entirely for the Lord, considering that:

1. The Lord has forgiven him all the sins that he had committed in his unconverted days;
2. The Lord has been even more merciful in forgiving the many sins that he committed after he was converted (including the ones he committed knowingly);
3. The Lord has promised never to remember his past sins and follies any more;
4. The Lord has covered his sins from the eyes of others, thus preserving his dignity;
5. The Lord does not listen to the accusations that Satan or any of Satan's agents (who know about his past failures) make against him;
6. The Lord has blessed him again and again in ways that he did not deserve;
7. The Lord is always on his side against Satan.

Such love breaks even the hardest heart and makes it willing to live utterly and only for God henceforth. We do not give ourselves to the Lord because He threatens us with fire and judgment. No. It is God's immense kindness that wins our hearts. That is God's way.

The man who had received one talent buried his talent, because he had thought his master to be "a hard and exacting man" (*Luke 19:21*). That was not the truth but because he believed it, he wasted his life. So also is it with many believers who consider God to be hard and exacting and demanding. They waste their earthly lives. In the day of judgment, they will bring forth their wasted lives and talents and show them to God.

God is not a spoilsport. "He rejoices over us with shouts of joy" (*Zephaniah 3:17*). He longs to be gracious and merciful to us, and to give us the very best in life. He only gives good and perfect gifts and He is more kind and loving than the best father that there ever was on earth. He gives good things to His children – and above all, the gift of the Holy Spirit. He desires to make our lives glorious in every possible way.

We must not allow Satan to paint a wrong picture of God to us. Nor must we allow Satan to portray a wrong picture of God to others through us. Those who imagine God to be a hard and austere person usually end up being hard and austere towards their marriage partners and their children, and towards other human beings as well.

We must be so convinced of God's forgiveness, that Satan cannot even try to accuse us any more, or make us feel condemned.

The secret of the overcomers, (who are mentioned again and again in the book of Revelation), is described in *Revelation 12:11*:

> "They overcame him (Satan – and his accusations – see *verse 10*) because of the blood of the Lamb, and because of the word of their testimony, and they did not love their life even unto death".

Notice the order here: They were first convinced that the blood of Christ had cleansed them. Then they told Satan what the blood of Christ had done for them. That was "the word of their testimony". Only after that did they take up the cross and follow Jesus ("They did not love their life even unto death"). That order must never be reversed. It is impossible to follow Jesus if we haven't been freed totally from condemnation first.

We are not going to be more holy by looking inside ourselves all the time and seeing how rotten we are. No. We are to run the race "looking unto Jesus", and not looking inside ourselves (*Hebrews 12:1, 2*).

God's Word is like a mirror (*James 1:23*). And God has given us that mirror so that the Holy Spirit might first show us the glory of Jesus through it – and not our own rottenness (See *2 Corinthians 3:18*). As we see the glory of Jesus more and more, we will naturally see how unlike Him we are, in area after area. But that will not discourage us, for the Spirit has also come to transform us into the likeness of Christ.

Let us then use the one talent (the one life) that God has given us to produce ten talents for Him.

14

Warnings to the Church for the Last Days

"The forces (of the antichrist) will defile the holy place and put a stop to the daily sacrifices... He will flatter those who disregard the covenant of God, and thus win them over to his side.

"But the people who know their God will be strong and do great things. And those with spiritual understanding will have a wide ministry of teaching in those days. But they will be in constant danger, many of them dying by fire and sword, or being jailed and robbed.

"Eventually these pressures will subside, and some ungodly men will come, pretending to offer a helping hand, only to take advantage of them. And some who are the most gifted in the things of God will stumble in those days and fall. (*Daniel 11:31–35* - TLB).

This is a passage that refers to the last days, and so there are many warnings that can be found therein for the church – for the spirit of the antichrist will be found even within the church (*1 John 2:18, 19*).

Defiling the Church with Impurity

The spirit of the antichrist seeks to "defile the holy place" (*verse 31*). There is tremendous opposition to the message of holiness and righteousness from Satan. The spirit of the antichrist also encourages "disregard of the covenant" (*verse 32*). The new covenant promises a life of victory over sin. But the antichrist tells believers that it is impossible to live such a life.

The main reason why our own ministry as a church has been opposed in the last two decades throughout India, has been because we have preached holiness and righteousness. We have proclaimed the fact that "sin need not be master over us any longer" (*Romans 6:14*), that "those who love money cannot love God" (*Luke 16:13*), that "those who are angry with and despise others are guilty enough to go to hell" (*Matthew 5:22*), that "those who lust after women with their eyes are also in danger of perishing in hell"

(*Matthew 5:28, 29*), etc. Since these words of Jesus are unpalatable to the vast majority of believers, they have opposed us.

We have stood against the unScriptural salary system for Christian workers (something that was unheard of in the first century) and the unScriptural begging for money that characterises Christian work in India. This has earned us the wrath of those who make a living through their preaching, and who build their private empires thereby.

We have also stood against personality-cults in the church, popery, denominationalism, Western domination of churches in India, and the unhealthy dependence on Western leadership that has hindered the development of the church here. This has infuriated the cultistic groups.

Satan's aim is to corrupt God's sanctuary in one way or the other. He places his "forces" (*Daniel 11:31*) within the church, in order to destroy God's work from within. The history of Christendom reveals how these forces have succeeded in corrupting group after group, and movement after movement, through all these 20 centuries.

> The main reason for the church's failure has been that the watchmen whom God appointed in the church did not remain alert and awake. How did Satan succeed in putting these watchmen to sleep? In some cases, by making them afraid to speak the truth lest they offend some people – especially the rich and the influential. In some other cases, by making them wife-pleasers, and lovers of money and of good food.

In some cases, the watchmen themselves got tired of facing constant opposition to their message, as they sought to maintain God's standards in the church. And so they toned down their messages to please men.

In *Hebrews 12:3*, we are told to consider Jesus "Who endured such hostility by sinners against Himself, so that we may not grow weary and lose heart". Who were these sinners who opposed Jesus? They were not the prostitutes or the murderers or the thieves in Israel. Nor were they the Romans or the Greeks. No. The sinners who opposed Jesus constantly, were the Bible-thumping preachers and religious leaders in Israel. They were jealous of Jesus and finally killed Him.

If we follow Jesus, we will face opposition from the same group of people even today. Our greatest opposition will come from the preachers who have lowered God's standards and corrupted the church. These will be Satan's chief agents to oppose us. It is very easy for us to get tired of facing this constant opposition, and to get discouraged.

Satan tries to "wear down the saints of God through persecution" (*Daniel 7:25*). The only way to overcome is by looking at the example of Jesus Who faced opposition constantly, until He was killed by His enemies. We too must be willing to "be faithful unto death". Any preacher who is unwilling to face opposition until the end of his life, will end up as an ear-tickling preacher, who will "flatter people to win them over to his side" (*Daniel 11:32*), and end his days as a compromising Balaam.

Our calling as a church is to preserve God's standards at any cost in our midst. We have to be on guard against the forces of the antichrist at all times. Paul had preserved the church in Ephesus in purity, by God's grace, during the three years that he was there. But he told the elders when he was leaving that he was certain that corruption would come in, after his departure (*Acts 20:29–31*). And sure enough, it did, as we read in the Second letter to the Ephesians (*Revelation 2:1–5*).

The Daily Sacrifice

We read further in *Daniel 11:31*, that one of the things that the antichrist will put an end to is "THE DAILY SACRIFICE".

Jesus constantly spoke to His disciples of a daily sacrifice – a daily sacrifice that he Himself had in His life: "If anyone will come after me let him deny himself and take up his cross DAILY..." (*Luke 9:23*).

This message has been eliminated by Satan from Christendom. And so the holy place has been corrupted. When the preaching of the cross disappears from any church, sin and worldliness soon take over.

The way into the most holy place lies through the rent veil (the crucified flesh). There is no other way to dwell with God, The Most Holy One. That was the way for Jesus – and there is no other way for us either.

Did you take up the cross yesterday? Maybe you did. But that was sufficient only for the evil appointed for you to face yesterday (*Matthew 6:34*).

Today is another day. And you have to offer your body and your self-will as a sacrifice again today. Today you have to die to your lusts, to your anger, to your pride, to your love of money, to your love of man's honour, to your bitterness etc. These lusts are still present in your flesh, and will be with you as long as you live. That is why you need to have "a daily sacrifice", right until the end of your earthly life.

Is there a daily sacrifice in your life?

If not, the spirit of the antichrist has certainly deceived you.

Jesus was anointed with the Spirit at the same time as He was baptized in water. Jesus being immersed in the River Jordan symbolised His accepting death and burial. This was to teach us that the way to live under the Spirit's anointing was by accepting death to Self.

In baptism, we are pushed into the water in God's Name, and we accept it, knowing that the one who pushes us into the water will also lift us out of it. So must it be when we face situations in life where we are pushed down and oppressed in any way. We must recognise that God is "delivering us over to death for Jesus' sake" in such situations (*2 Corinthians 4:10, 11*). And when we accept death to our self-life, we can be certain that the God Who led us into that death will raise us up too.

If those who had been baptised in the Holy Spirit in past decades had maintained the daily sacrifice in their lives and in their churches, they would have had tremendous power and influence for God in our land. But Satan succeeded in sidetracking most of them, by leading them to emphasise speaking in tongues, healing, working-up of the emotions, and various forms of religious activity, instead of the way of the cross.

The only way to overcome Satan, and to preserve the power of God in our lives, in our homes and in our churches, is by maintaining the daily sacrifice at any cost, without any compromise whatsoever.

Those who have read the HIDDEN TREASURES paper over the years have read this message of "taking up the cross daily" again and again. But very few among them have been gripped by it.

Herod "used to enjoy listening to John the Baptist" (*Mark 6:20*), because John the Baptist was a fiery preacher, interesting to listen to, unlike the boring Pharisees. Many enjoy reading HIDDEN

TREASURES for the same reason. But they do not become any more spiritual than King Herod!!

There are some who read HIDDEN TREASURES in order to get fresh points – which they don't find in other books – for their sermons. Since God Himself has said that He is against those who steal messages from others (*Jeremiah 23:30*), there is very little hope for such preachers – who are always looking out for points for their sermons, instead of judging themselves and allowing God to speak to their own need.

If, for example, you are offended because someone did not give you the respect that you think you deserve, or because you were not given some position of responsibility in the church, that is a clear indication that the daily sacrifice has been eliminated from your life. If you die to Self, you will never get offended with anything or anyone at any time.

True and False Prophets

We read in *Daniel 11:32*, that those who are influenced by the spirit of the antichrist will use smooth words (flattery) to draw people to themselves. The one unmistakable characteristic of every false prophet in history has been flattery. And the one unmistakable characteristic of every true prophet has been rebuke. False prophets flatter people in order to win them to their group, or to build their own kingdoms, or to get honour, or to get money, etc. Many of these false prophets correspond faithfully with people, in order to retain their personal hold over them. Their letters will not however contain words of rebuke and correction (like the letters of the Lord and of the apostles contain – as we read in *Revelation 2 & 3* and the epistles). They will only contain words of appreciation, commendation and flattery.

Remember that smooth words will only defile your heart with pride and self-satisfaction. Words of rebuke on the other hand will cleanse your heart and make it pure. Jesus said "Those whom I love, I reprove and I discipline" (*Revelation 3:19*). Rebuke is one mark of Divine love.

When God sends a prophet into our midst, to rebuke us, that is a proof of the fact that God loves us. When God forsakes a church, it will "no longer have a prophet in its midst" (*Psalm 74:1, 9*) to rebuke it. Instead, it will have preachers who preach smooth words (*2 Timothy 4:3, 4*). That is a sad condition for any of God's people to be in.

In *Revelation 2 and 3*, we see that even though five of the seven churches there were in a bad shape, yet the Lord had not forsaken them as yet. The proof of this is seen in the fact that He sent a prophet (John the apostle) to rebuke and correct them through his letters.

John had strong words even for the elders – words such as, "You have left your first love…You are spiritually dead…You are wretched and poor and blind and naked". If those elders and those churches did not respond to those words of rebuke, and repent, they would be forsaken.

Once the Lord "takes away the lampstand" (*Revelation 2:5*), He will not send His prophets to rebuke that church any more. The false prophets will then take over, and smooth words will be heard regularly at the meetings, Sunday after Sunday!! This has happened in church after church, in generation after generation, throughout these twenty centuries. And it is happening all around us today.

It is at such a time, that there is a great need for those "who know God, who are strong, and who will do great things for Him" (*verse 32*). Because they know God, they will fear no man. But there is only one way to know God – and that is through the daily sacrifice. The veil has to be rent if we are to enter into the Most Holy Place where God dwells. So don't ever allow the daily sacrifice to be taken away from your life.

If your husband or wife treats you badly – DIE. When you suffer unrighteously – DIE. If your brothers betray you and hate you – DIE. As you die to your Self-life, you will get to know God and Jesus better.

The Right Attitude Towards Our Enemies

Even if people scheme against you to harm you, you don't have to worry. God will take care of you and He will deal with your enemies as well.

"He Who keeps you will neither slumber nor sleep." (Psalm 121:3, 4)

And since God is constantly awake, we can afford to go to sleep.

In the book of Esther, we read of Haman and his wife staying awake a whole night, scheming and plotting against Mordecai and preparing a 75-foot gallows to hang Mordecai on. (A 10-foot gallows is actually sufficient to hang a man. But they made a 75-foot one, so that everyone in the city would be able to see the hanging, so that Mordecai would be humiliated even further). But Mordecai was fast asleep, and God took care of him. The gallows that Haman prepared for Mordecai finally became the very gallows on which Haman himself was hung (*Esther 5:14; 7:10*). God is an expert at turning the tables on Satan.

Your enemies may go from house to house, speaking evil against you, scheming your harm, and even seeking to "hang" you. But you need not fear. They themselves will hang on the gallows they prepare for you.

We have seen time and again, that those who have secretly schemed against us in the church have had the tables turned against them always. We haven't found any delight in seeing such brothers hang on the gallows that they prepared for us. We have always forgiven them and blessed them, and hoped that they would repent and find their way back into the church. But God's laws cannot be changed:

"The man who sets a trap for others will get caught in it himself. If you roll a boulder down on someone, it will roll back and crush you. God catches the wise in their own craftiness" (*Proverbs 26:27* - TLB; *1 Corinthians 3:19*).

No-one can avoid reaping what he has sown.
So what should we do, when people plan to hang us?
SLEEP!! For "God gives His beloved sleep" (*Psalm 127:2*).

In *Acts 12*, we read of Herod imprisoning Peter, planning to kill him the next morning. But God gave Peter sound sleep that night (*verse 6*). The angel of the Lord then went down, woke Peter up, released him and sent him home (*verse 7*). But that is not the end of the story. The angel of the Lord paid a second visit to earth, and this time he smote Herod and killed him (*verse 23*)!! God turns the tables on Satan again and again.

Judas Iscariot betrayed Jesus. But what happened to Judas? He died even before Jesus died (*Matthew 27:5*).

If you fear God, you need not fear the Hamans or the Herods – or even the Judas Iscariots – who plot your harm.

No-one can fight against God – or against God's church – and succeed. Many have tried to do that in past years – but they have all failed, without a single exception. We are on the victory side.

Persecution is Inevitable

That does not mean that we will never be persecuted or killed. We read in *Daniel 11:33*, that in the last days, godly people will be attacked, imprisoned and killed. True servants of God are always persecuted.

James was killed by King Herod (*Acts 12:2*). No angel came to set him free. Abel was killed. Every true prophet in the Old Testament was persecuted (*Acts 7:52*). John the Baptist was beheaded. Jesus was crucified. Stephen was stoned to death. Paul was beheaded. History tells us that Peter himself was finally crucified – and no angel came to rescue him then. As far as we know, all the apostles, except John, were killed. Many God-fearing missionaries have been killed in heathen lands.

The Bible clearly teaches that the church will go through the great tribulation before Jesus comes, and that many of God's finest saints will be killed during that time (*Revelation 13:7*). Some of God's finest saints have been killed in Communist lands even in our lifetime.

God's purposes are different for each person. But one thing is certain: If you desire only to glorify God in your earthly life and to walk in the will of God, you will be immortal until your life's work is done.

"Those who have spiritual understanding will have a wide teaching ministry in the last days.... Wise leaders of God's people will share their wisdom with many others." (*Daniel 11:33* - TLB & GNT).

On the other hand, there will also be many in the last days "whom the Lord hates, who go around sowing discord among the brothers" (*Proverbs 6:16–19*). We do not fight against such people, because we refuse to fight with flesh and blood (*Ephesians 6:12*). We fight only with Satan, and we leave it to the angel of the Lord to deal with all our human opponents.

Many years ago I decided that I would never fight with any human being concerning any matter – and I have never regretted that decision. When anyone comes to quarrel with me, I either keep quiet, or get up and go away. When people accuse me by letter, I do not reply. It is sheer waste of time to reply to such people. I only forgive them, bless them, love them, AND LEAVE THEM ALONE. I want to concentrate my energies on fighting Satan. I have realised that God can deal with these agents of the Accuser better than I can. Vengeance belongs to Him (*Romans 12:19*).

We read further in *Daniel 11:34* that "many will join with these evil men in their hypocrisy". Many will become hypocrites in a time of persecution. They will act like wholehearted brothers when in the midst of the church, and talk about judging themselves and taking up the cross etc. But when they are in the midst of their worldly friends and their unconverted relatives, they will seek man's honour and behave with them and speak with them in such a way as to be accepted by them.

There are many believers today who having a root of bitterness within them have defiled many others in the church (*Hebrews 12:15*). But God has been long-suffering with all of them, and so they are all still in the church. But in due course, they will all be exposed (if they don't repent), and then they too will fall away, like others before them.

If we know God, we will remain "rooted and grounded in love" (*Ephesians 3:17*) – and rooted in the church too. If others hate us and betray us and kick us out of their houses, we will forgive them, love them and wait for another opportunity to serve them. And when that opportunity arises, we will be quick to grasp it, to bless them to the best of our ability. No-one will be able to make us evil. If another person's evil behaviour makes us evil, then we too become servants of Satan like him.

We are told that in the last days, "even those with insight will fall" (*Daniel 11:35*). But if they humble themselves and judge themselves, there will be hope even for them. They can then be "refined, purged and made pure" (*verse 35*). Those who don't judge themselves however will fall into Satan's hands, even though they had insight and understanding of God's ways at one time. Today is the day of grace, and those who repent and judge themselves can still ascend to great heights spiritually. But you have to be honest and you have to walk in the light.

This refining and purging will carry on until "the end of time" (*Daniel 11:35*), so that God can fulfil His goal of conforming us to the likeness of Christ. So we must not expect an easy time on earth, until Jesus comes. In the world we shall have tribulation – CONTINUOUSLY.

A Daniel-Ministry and a Lucifer-Ministry

Daniel (who wrote this prophecy) was one of those men whom God could use in his generation. When he was a 17-year old young man, "he determined in his heart not to defile himself" (*Daniel 1:8*). And when Hananiah, Mishael and Azariah saw young Daniel taking a stand for the Lord, they too got the boldness to stand for the Lord themselves (*Daniel 1:11*). They did not have the courage to stand on their own. But they became bold when they saw Daniel's stand. There are many people like that today, who do not have the boldness to stand for the Lord alone, but who are waiting for a Daniel to take a stand. Then they will join him.

> Will you be such a Daniel? Will you say, "I will not defile myself. I will not seek to please the king, or the commander, or any backslidden elder, or anyone. I shall stand 100% for what the Word of God says."

There is a great need for a Daniel-ministry in our land today – men and women who will "lead many to righteousness" (*Daniel 12:4*). That verse does not refer to preachers who preach about righteousness, but to those who lead others to righteousness – by word and example.

We read in Scripture of yet another ministry – and this is the exact opposite of this "Daniel-ministry" – a "Lucifer-ministry".

In *Revelation 12:4*, we read that Lucifer succeeded in getting millions of angels to follow him in his rebellion against God. Why did God permit Lucifer to lead so many angels astray? So that heaven could be purged of all the disgruntled and rebellious angels. Their evil hearts would not have been exposed, had not a Lucifer arisen in their midst to lead them in their rebellion against God.

And so, even today, God will allow brothers and sisters to have a Lucifer-ministry in the church. They will be permitted by God to go around from house to house backbiting, accusing, telling lies and speaking evil, so that all the disgruntled, rebellious and worldly believers in the church can be identified, exposed, gathered together and taken out of the church – so that the Body of Christ can be purified.

God will not stop those who are engaged in such a Lucifer-ministry from moving around the church, any more than He stopped the original Lucifer in heaven, millions of years ago. That is Divine wisdom.

We are never to fight with such brothers and sisters either. God Himself will preserve the church, and at the right time, He will destroy those who defile the church (*1 Corinthians 3:17*). But God is long-suffering and waits many years before He judges – because He does not want anyone to perish, but wants everyone to repent. In Noah's time, He waited 120 years. But when God does judge, His judgment will be severe.

It is foolish therefore to boast that a church has never had a split. There was a split in heaven itself, among the angels, right at the beginning. Such splits are necessary, for "there must be divisions, so that those who are approved (by God) can become manifest" (*1 Corinthians 11:19*).

The light has to be separated from the darkness. That is not a split. It is a cleansing. Without it, God's testimony on earth will be corrupted.

All of us can have either a Daniel-ministry – building unity and fellowship in the church – or a Lucifer-ministry – sowing discord.

We cannot be neutral. Jesus said that those who do not gather with Him are scattering people away from Him. There are only two ministries in the church – gathering and scattering (*Matthew 12:30*).

May we have grace and wisdom to live in these last days, as God wants us to live, so that the church can be built as a pure testimony in every place for the glory of God's Name.

15

What a Happy Year it will Be!

*"The Sabbath (and so also each of God's laws) was made to benefit man,
and not man to benefit the Sabbath"* (Mark 2:27).

All of God's laws are meant to make us happy. God did not create man because He needed creatures to keep some laws that He had already made. No. On the contrary He made the laws after creating man – so as to make man supremely and perpetually happy.

God made Adam in the second half of the sixth day. Thus the seventh day (the Sabbath) was man's very first day of existence. Adam did not have to work for six days before getting a Sabbath. God in his goodness gave him a day of rest first before asking him to work for six days. That first day was to be a day spent at rest and in fellowship with God. Out of that fellowship with his Creator, was to flow Adam's service for God during the next six days. This is the pattern that we are called to follow – for this is how God intended things to be for man, from the beginning.

The Bible begins with the words, "In the beginning God...". And that must be true of everything that we do in our lives: God must be in the beginning of our every activity. We must begin everything as Adam did – entering into the rest of fellowship with God, before we seek to serve Him.

Martha served the Lord. But because she served Him with a spirit of agitation, the Lord rebuked her (*Luke 10:38–42*). Mary however was at rest, and this is what the Lord said was "the one thing needful".

Many serve the Lord today, but they do not know the Sabbath rest of fellowship with God in their inner beings. Thus they serve the Lord in a legalistic spirit and "never cease from their own works" (*Hebrews 4:10*).

The New Testament speaks of "a Sabbath rest for the people of God" (*Hebrews 4:9*). What does this new-covenant Sabbath refer to?

Under the old covenant, God gave the Jews many types of Sabbaths. The weekly Sabbath is well-known. There were however some lesser known Sabbaths as well. One was the Sabbath year that came at the end of every six years (*Leviticus 25:2–4*). Another was the fiftieth-year Sabbath that came at the end of every seven Sabbath years (after every 49 years). This fiftieth year Sabbath was called "the year of jubilee" (*Leviticus 25:8–12*).

In the year of jubilee, the Israelites were "to proclaim liberty throughout the land to all enslaved debtors", and it was to be "a time for the cancelling of all debts" (*Leviticus 25:10* - TLB).

The Lord had commanded the cancellation of all debts at the end of every seventh year as well, when "every creditor shall write, 'Paid in full', on any promissory note he holds...because the Lord has released everyone from his obligation" (Read *Deuteronomy 25:1–10* carefully).

God had a great interest in people releasing their debtors. This was why He instituted two Sabbath years – one every seventh year and one every fiftieth year – in which all debtors were to be released.

The Sabbath years were to be times of great blessing and joy. The word "jubilee" means "a shout of joy". The year of jubilee was to be a year full of joyous shouts – because every debt had been forgiven, and every debtor released. Therefore the Lord told the Israelites concerning that year, "What a happy year it will be for you" (*Leviticus 25:11* - TLB).

Now, under the new covenant we celebrate the Sabbath day every day of the week, for every day is holy unto the Lord.

And we celebrate the Sabbath year every year – for every year is a year of jubilee – a year of rejoicing in which we release and forgive all who have harmed us and cheated us. Thus every single year of our lives can be happy – for every year is meant to be a year of jubilee for us.

In the year of jubilee, the Lord commanded that "each of you shall return to his family" (*Leviticus 25:10b*). All who have been estranged from their brothers and sisters in the Body of Christ (due to whatever reason) must now return to the family of God.

This is God's command under the new covenant. Every debt (sin) must be forgiven, and every slave(the ones against whom we have some demands) must be released. This too is the Lord's command. Only then will each year be a happy year for us.

God has forgiven us so much that to forgive others from our hearts is the very least that we can do as an expression of our gratitude to Him Who loved us and gave Himself for us.

It is written of King Hezekiah, after he was miraculously healed by the Lord from a serious sickness, that he "gave no return for the benefit he received" (*2 Chronicles 32:24, 25*). He did not give back to God according to the measure in which God had blessed Him.

What about us? Have we given back to the Lord in the same measure as we have been blessed by Him? Have we forgiven others as freely as God forgave us? EVERYONE? Is there even one left out, still unforgiven?

Because King Hezekiah acted in pride and ingratitude, the next fifteen years of his life were the worst period of his whole life. He produced a son during that time (Manasseh) who became the worst king that Judah ever had (*2 Kings 21:11*). Hezekiah who began his reign in a spirit of revival, ended it in grief.

When we don't forgive and release others, the remaining years of our life on earth will be really bad.

Our calling is to be merciful to others just as God has been merciful to us. That phrase, "JUST AS GOD HAS BEEN TO US" is the motto we must keep in mind at all times in our dealings with all human beings.

We have received much freely from the Lord. Then let us give freely to others as well (*Matthew 10:8*) – not in a miserly or stingy way, but liberally and with a large heart. If we are tight-fisted and demanding in our dealings with others, God will be tight-fisted and demanding in His dealings with us as well (See *Psalm 18:25, 26*).

We must never lose the wonder of the forgiveness that the Lord has granted us so freely. OUR WHOLE LIFE MUST NOW BE LIVED AS AN EXPRESSION OF GRATITUDE TO THE LORD FOR ALL THAT HE DID FOR US ON CALVARY'S CROSS.

Under the Law it was through threats of judgment that people served the Lord. But under grace, it is to be through the power of gratitude.

In *Matthew 18:23–35*, Jesus told His disciples a parable of a kind king who had forgiven his servant a large debt of thirty crores rupees (Rs.300 million). That servant's debt was so large that he could never have repaid it in his own lifetime or for generations to come. So he should have been immensely grateful for the forgiveness that he had received.

But, he did not render to others in the same measure as he himself had received. He went out from his master's presence and immediately went to the house of another man who owed him sixty thousand rupees. Now, Rs.60,000 is certainly not a small sum of money that we can easily overlook. But it was a mere drop in the ocean compared to the Rs.300,000,000 that he had been forgiven! But what did this man do? He "grabbed the other man by the throat and demanded instant repayment". And when the other man could not repay, he had him arrested and jailed. This was reported to the king who immediately called for the unmerciful servant and calling him "an evil-hearted wretch", handed him over to the torturers, until he repaid the entire amount.

And then Jesus said, "So shall My Heavenly Father also do to you, if each of you does not forgive his brother from your heart" (*verse 35*).

That certainly teaches us that if we don't forgive others, God will withdraw the forgiveness that He once granted us and He will make us pay for the sins that He had once blotted out from His sight, and that He had once promised never to remember again. God's forgiving of our sins is always conditional on our CONTINUING TO forgive others.

The prayer that the Lord taught His disciples in *Matthew 6:9–13* is a prayer that was obviously meant to be prayed daily, since He taught us there to pray for our DAILY food. If that be the case, then this part of the prayer also must be one that must be prayed daily: "Forgive us our debts (sins), as we also have forgiven our debtors (those who have sinned against us)". We have to forgive others every day of our lives, because every day someone or the other will hurt us in some way (either consciously or unconsciously).

Jesus cancelled the certificate of debt that we had to God, and He destroyed the letters of accusation that the Law had against us, when He died on Calvary (*Colossians 2:14*). Have we done the same to our debtors? Or do we still retain letters to accuse others with, and memories of the wrongs that others have done to us in the past. If so, then God has no alternative but to hand us and our families over to the torturers (evil spirits) to harass us until we have learnt to forgive.

The king in this parable had wanted his servant to show mercy out of gratitude. It was only when the servant failed to act out of gratitude for the mercies that he himself had received, that the king adopted Method No. 2 – that of torture. It is the same with God. He desires primarily that we forgive others out of gratitude for what He has done for us. It is when we don't respond to that call of grace, then God places us under the Law, hoping that we will respond at least to the threats of the Law. Then He seeks to teach us to forgive others, by handing us over to the torturers. The reason why many believers never seem to be able to enter the Sabbath rest of God and are unsteady, unpredictable in their behaviour, often gloomy, long-faced, depressed and irritable is because they haven't forgiven others. The torturers are working on their spirit.

We must make a bonfire of the "letters of accusation" that we have carefully preserved to accuse others with. And we must determine with an inviolable determination that we will never, under any provocation, bring out old certificates of debt to charge others with at any time.

Under the old covenant they could have a happy year (a year of jubilee) only once every fifty years. How much better it is for us under the new covenant – for we can have a happy year every year of our lives.

An unforgiving spirit gradually begins to wish evil to those whom it has not forgiven. When you wish evil for another person, it is equivalent to cursing him. We read in *Galatians 3:13* that Jesus took the curse of the whole world upon Himself. So when we curse another, we are actually cursing Jesus Himself who took everyone's curse. Think of that the next time Satan tempts you to wish evil for someone else or his children.

If the Pharisees who brought the woman caught in adultery to Jesus, had started stoning that poor woman, Jesus would have stood in front of that woman and received the stones Himself and said, "Kill Me first". That is what He did for us on Calvary. He stood in front of us and received the "stones" that we should have received. The spirit of Christ is the spirit of the new covenant, and it is the exact opposite of the spirit of the Pharisees. Only one who has the Spirit of Christ can enter into a lifetime of perpetual happiness.

A true story entitled "Love's Atom Bomb", was published some years ago about a godly Christian in Korea whose young son was shot dead by a Communist youth. That godly father went and sought out his son's murderer and not only forgave him but adopted him as his own son and brought him up. Such a man certainly understood "the new and living way" far better than many who know only the doctrine and the Scripture-references! Jesus did not teach the way as a doctrine. He walked it all through His life. He loved those who hated Him to such an extent, that He gave His life-blood to save them. This is the new and living way.

We are now called to follow in Jesus' footsteps – not putting a curse on others by wishing evil for them, but by blessing those who curse us. The world is full of people who wish evil for others and who go around cursing and complaining and speaking evil of others. Let us go around instead doing good and blessing and releasing people everywhere we go in this year of jubilee!

In *Galatians 3:13, 14*, we are told that since Christ has taken our curse, we can receive "the blessing of Abraham" upon us now. This is possible for us through being continuously filled with the Holy Spirit.

In John's gospel, Jesus used the symbol of water to describe three levels of spiritual development possible through the Holy Spirit:

Level 1: In *John 3:5*, He spoke of being "born of water and the Spirit". This is "the cup of salvation" (*Psalm 116:13*), with which we begin our Christian lives. With this cup of water, we are cleansed and brought into God's kingdom as his children.

Level 2: In *John 4:14*, Jesus went further and spoke of that cup becoming "a well (spring) of water". This is a deeper experience of the Holy Spirit, where all our inner longings are met by Him, so that we live in perpetual victory and joy, lacking nothing. A man who has a well in his own compound is not dependent on the city corporation's water supply. No outsider can turn off his water supply, for he has the source of water within his own compound. This is how it is with the Christian who has found the secret of perpetual abundance in Christ. No-one outside of him can cut off his supply of joy or peace or victory (*John 16:22*).

Level 3: In *John 7:38*, Jesus went still further and said that the well would now become a river, and many rivers, flowing out of the believer. This is a picture of overflowing abundance. Such a believer is able to quench the thirst of many needy people around him. Whereas a well satisfies only our own longings, rivers of living water make us a blessing to many people, wherever we go.

The blessing with which God blessed Abraham was, "I will bless you...and in you ALL THE FAMILIES of the earth shall be blessed" (*Genesis 12:2, 3*). This is the blessing that can now be ours through the Holy Spirit (*Galatians 3:14*).

When God blesses us to the point of rivers flowing out of us, many families in many parts of the country and even in the whole world can be blessed through us.

Only a cursed person hurts and injures other people wherever he goes. This is how most of the children of Adam live. They only know how to wish evil for others, hurt them with their rude remarks and defile them with their backbiting. Unfortunately even many "believers" live like this, proving thereby, either that their conversion was false or that they have backslidden to the point of having lost their salvation.

The good news of the gospel is that we can be saved from such a miserable existence. We can now have rivers of living water flowing out through us constantly, and be a blessing to every family that we meet.

We can be merciful to others just as God has been merciful to us.
We can release others just as God has released us.
We can bless others just as God has blessed us.
We can give freely to others just as God has freely given to us.
We can be large-hearted to others just as God has been to us.

A.W. Tozer in his article Five Decisions For Spiritual Power says:

"If you are really serious about your spiritual development – the gaining of new joy, new power and new life – then you should

make certain decisions in your heart concerning your life, and proceed to keep them.

"One decision is: Never pass on anything about anybody else that will hurt him.

"'Love covers a multitude of sins' (1 Peter 4:8). The talebearer has no place in God's favour. If you know something that would hinder or hurt the reputation of one of God's children, bury it forever. Let God take care of it. 'With what judgment you judge, you will be judged' (Matthew 7:2)."

"If you want God to be good to you, you must be good to His children. The rules of our Father's table demand that you don't tell stories about others who are sitting around that same table with you, no matter what their denomination, their nationality or their background." (From the book THE BEAUTY OF HOLINESS)

It will be a good thing if all of us make that decision today – never to pass on anything about another that will hurt him or his reputation – and keep that decision, not just for the rest of this year but for the rest of our lives. Those who have lived by that decision in past years have found that when they discarded the worthless from their daily conversation, and spoke only what was edifying and profitable, God in turn, fulfilled His promise, and made them His spokesmen – His mouth (*Jeremiah 15:19*).

Although Judas Iscariot was a deceiver and a betrayer, yet Jesus never spoke about him to the other eleven disciples in all the three years that he was with them. That was why none of them knew at the last supper who the betrayer was. Jesus never indulged in gossip. He may have spoken to Judas personally. But He never spoke of him behind his back, until God Himself exposed Judas. We too must be patient for God to expose evil people. He is well able to do that without our having to help Him with our backbiting!!

When we deal with sinners and backsliders, we can behave towards them either like the father of the prodigal son, or like the elder brother of the prodigal son (*Luke 15:11–32*).

In that parable, the house is a picture of the church. The father is a picture, not only of God, but also of a true father in the church. And the elder brother is a picture of the Pharisees who are found in every church on the face of the earth. God uses sinners and backsliders (like the prodigal son)to expose the Pharisees in the church.

Pharisees may have righteousness, but they have neither goodness nor humility. They find it difficult to accept a backslider as an equal. They feel that he must be put in the servant's quarters for a few months on probation when he comes back. God however doesn't do that, for He is not a Pharisee. He clothes the repentant sinner with the robe (of Christ's righteousness) as soon as he comes back. He gives him the ring (the anointing of the Holy Spirit) immediately on his return. And He gives the sinner a place at His right hand at once.

Jesus, Who never sinned even once during His entire life on earth, entered paradise, after His death on Calvary, with a repentant thief who had spent his entire life on earth in sin. Only grace can accomplish such a wonder. But Pharisees don't understand such grace, and so they become hard and unforgiving. Thus they destroy themselves. Remember that, at the end of the parable, the elder son is outside the father's house – having lost his salvation because of an unmerciful attitude towards his younger brother. That is the ultimate end of all who despise others.

The younger son, through all his folly and sin, finally came to see his own need, became poor in spirit, and inherited his father's kingdom. The elder son however, never came to such poverty of spirit, because he never saw his own need. He only saw the sins of others. And so he was lost, despite his claim to have faithfully kept all his father's commandments (*Luke 15:29*). A legalistic obedience can lead believers to such Pharisaism that their last state becomes worse than their first.

This year – and every year – can be a happy year for all of us, if we release everyone who owes us anything, or who has hurt or harmed us in any way. Bury those grudges permanently and be merciful to all men and thus make a new beginning with the Lord today.

16

Will You Shrink Away from the Lord When He Returns?

"Abide in Him, so that when he appears, we may have confidence and not shrink away from Him in shame at His coming." (1 John 2:28).

The coming of the Lord is something that all believers are looking forward to with great joy. Why then will some believers have to shrink away from the Lord's presence in shame when He returns?

There could be many reasons for that. But I want to point out one.

In *John 8:1–12*, we read of the Pharisees bringing a woman caught in adultery to Jesus, accusing her, and then shrinking away from His presence in shame.

Why did they shrink away from the presence of the Lord? Because Jesus told them that the first person to begin throwing stones should be the one who has no sin in him.

Suddenly they realised, in the glaring light of Jesus' presence, that what they had accused the woman of, they were all guilty of themselves.

In *Romans 2:1*, we read,

"Therefore you are without excuse, every man of you who passes judgment, for in that you judge another, you condemn yourself; for you who judge practise the same things."

When we stand before the Lord, we will discover this amazing fact: That every single matter in which we ever pointed a finger at another, we were guilty of ourselves, in some measure, at some time, in our lives.

God's light will be so bright in that day, that we will see clearly that we ourselves committed the very same things that we accused others of doing. It is this that will make every believer who has accused others shrink away from the Lord in shame.

It will also become evident then that such believers were also Pharisees themselves.

Many believers are so sharp-eyed that they pass judgment on even the smallest words and actions of others. They criticise even the way others pray, testify or preach. There will always be something imperfect in the best things that anyone does, because we all have a flesh in which nothing good dwells. But the one who has an accusing spirit does not recognise any faults in himself, but only in others.

We will "know ourselves" fully – the full extent of our selfishness and our pride – only in the perfect light of God, when our Lord returns (*1 Corinthians 13:12*). If we could see ourselves more fully now, we would never again judge or criticise anything in another person, for we would see that we have the same defect ourselves.

The more we have seen the corruption within our own flesh, the less we will find fault with others around us.

Consider this: Isn't it true that you would have to be a first-class hypocrite to criticise adultery in another, if you had just committed adultery yourself that very morning? It would take a hard and insensitive father to criticise his child for spilling its milk on the floor, if the father himself had spilt his cup of coffee two minutes earlier!!

Why then do we judge and criticise others? Because we imagine that we are incapable of ever doing such things ourselves.

That was why the Pharisees were so bold to come to Jesus with the woman caught in adultery. But when they came into Jesus' presence, His light exposed that very same sin in their own hearts. Then "they shrank away from Him in shame".

This will be the fate of all who have judged and criticised others, when the Lord returns: They will shrink away from the Lord in shame, when they see the depth of corruption in their own flesh, and how they had judged and criticised the same things in others.

It is very easy for any of us to see where another person is behaving selfishly or in stubbornness or in pride.

Maybe you have often said, "So-and-so is a very selfish person", or "So-and-so is a very stubborn, self-willed person" or "So-and-so is a very proud person". And what you said may have been absolutely true.

But if you have ever said such words about another, you can be certain that when Christ returns, God will show you greater areas of selfishness, stubbornness, self-will, and pride in your own life.

And when you see that in that day, you too (like those Pharisees) will shrink away from the Lord's presence in shame – for having been so self-righteous as to judge others for much smaller degrees of these sins.

Do we realise that there is some form of these evils in every single one of us – which we cannot see?

If we realised this, we would be very slow to judge others for these things. We would assume that those others, whom we are judging, also (like us) cannot see their own selfishness, stubbornness and pride.

But unfortunately the flesh is such that we don't make such merciful allowances for others, where we make plenty of allowance for ourselves.

That is why God's Word says that "judgment will be merciless on the one who has shown no mercy himself" (*James 2:13*).

And that is why Jesus said, "Judge not" (*Matthew 7:1*).

We have to be careful even when we say, "I have forgiven all those who have harmed me" – for there is pride and conceit even in the very feeling that others have harmed us.

Peter asks, "Who can harm you?" (*1 Peter 3:13*). The answer is obviously, "No-one" – because as Paul said, "all things work together for good to those who love God" (*Romans 8:28*). If everything works together for our good, how can anyone ever harm us?

Yet there are multitudes of believers today who feel that some people did harm them and their families. What shall we say to such believers, in the light of God's clear Word? Just this: "Let God be found true, even though every man – including you – be found a liar." (*Romans 3:3*).

I have heard self-righteous believers in the church testifying that while others have harmed them and their children, they have forgiven them. They have obviously congratulated themselves for their Christ-likeness!! There is enormous pride however in such a testimony, for what such believers are actually saying (if I were to paraphrase their words) is, "I am surrounded by people who have behaved like the Devil towards me – even in the church. But I (spiritual man/woman that I am) have behaved like Jesus towards them and forgiven them. See how magnanimous and good I am!!"

Their testimony has reminded me of the nursery rhyme where Little Jack Horner puts his thumb into his pie, pulls out a plum and says, "What a good boy am I"!!. May God save the church from such Pharisees!

Holy-Spirit-given prophecy will always glorify Jesus (*Revelation 19:10*).

It is the spirit of Satan that points out one's own goodness and highlights it against the supposed evil of others!

Such believers may not be telling lies when they say that they have forgiven those who harmed them. But they obviously don't make allowance for the fact that those others may have done those things unconsciously. And further, they don't have any light on how much they themselves may have hurt those others in many other ways.

When the Lord returns, they will see that it is they themselves who had behaved like the Devil with their accusing spirit. And they will also see that they had harmed others much more than anyone had harmed them.

But such believers cannot smell the stink of their self-righteousness right now!! For Pharisaism can disguise itself even in the cloak of a merciful attitude towards others!! That is how deceptive the flesh is!

If any of you have been like that, I hope you will get a little light on your self-righteousness and pride, at least now, so that you can see how much your behaviour has been like the Devil's, in your judgmental and critical attitudes towards others.

If you haven't seen the evil of this matter until now, have you considered why you haven't seen it as yet? Here is the answer: It is because you are not pressing on to perfection. You are not hungering and thirsting after righteousness. You are not purifying yourself as Jesus is pure. And therefore you are not really ready for the coming of the Lord (according to *1 John 3:2, 3*). When the Lord comes suddenly, you will have to shrink away in shame from His presence.

It is good to ask the Lord to give you more light on yourself now, before it is too late.

One evidence of spiritual progress is that we regret some of the things that we did in the past – even what we did last year. That indicates that we are growing in wisdom. We may not have done anything evil. But we realise now that we could have done things a little more perfectly, and in a more Christ-like way. We did not sin consciously perhaps, but we did sin unconsciously, for anything un-Christlike is sin.

Therefore those who say that they look back over their lives without any regret, must be those who have not grown at all. They must be in the same spiritual state today that they were in when they were first converted. They loved money then. They love money now. They lost their temper then. And they lose their temper now. Yet they have no sorrow or regret over their actions and their way of life. How blind such people are! Yet they have been so quick to pass judgments on others! What regret will be theirs when Christ comes again.

One who preaches God's Word in the church, if he is progressing spiritually, will preach in a more Christ-like way every year. But this can happen only if he is judging himself – his motives, his words, his manner etc., – after each time that he preaches. Very, very few of those who preach God's Word judge themselves after their preaching. So they continue on in the same monotonous, boring way, without the anointing or grace or power of the Spirit upon their lives, year after year.

Hungry souls will travel hundreds of miles if they can find a man of God somewhere, who has the touch of heaven on his ministry and who is worth listening to – even as the multitudes travelled to the wilderness of Judea to hear John the Baptist, and as they travelled from all over Israel to hear Jesus, and as the crowds in many cities travelled long distances to hear the apostle Paul.

Those who are elders, have you realised how much you have bored others, when you have preached in the meetings without any spiritual preparation and without the anointing of the Spirit? Maybe you have spoken carelessly and lazily, without either thought or prayer, and then gone on preaching for forty long minutes in a meeting. And the long-suffering brothers and sisters in your church have endured this torture, without a word of complaint! O, how much you have sinned against them! And yet they have kept quiet. Have you recognised your sin?

In many assemblies, the elders are not feeding their flock, but instead boring them to death with their long, tiring sermons. It is good for all elders to judge themselves and to ask some of the other brothers for an honest opinion about themselves. Those who have lost the anointing should stop preaching and give the pulpit to some younger brother (like David) who has a fire and an anointing, instead of sitting (like King Saul) upon their thrones and hindering God's work.

How many of us have recognised that we must have unconsciously injured and hurt others, made demands on them, acted without consideration, taken advantage of the hospitality and goodness of others, written letters that wounded others, etc., without even realising it? And those others have suffered and borne with us, without even speaking a word to us about it.

How many of us have been thankful for the spoken and written ministry in the church that has preserved us from many sins that we would have fallen into long ago, if we had not had a place in the church?

How many of us have been thankful to God for our wives who have slogged away, day and night, serving us in multitudes of ways in our homes? We have taken so much for granted in our homes. How can we expect our children to be thankful to us, their parents, if we as husbands are not thankful for our wives. Our children have to learn such habits from us! Many husbands will discover when Christ returns, how evil and unthankful they were towards their wives. And many wives will discover in that day how evil and unthankful they were towards their husbands for all that their husbands did for them.

Have we even once expressed our thanks to God for our marriage-partners and our brothers and sisters? Yet how quick we have been to find fault with them, when we have seen even one mistake in them? And how quick we have been to forget all the good that they have done to us?

I remember hearing a story of a teacher who spread a large white sheet of paper with a small black dot in one corner, in front of his class of students once. He then asked the students what they saw. All of them said that they saw a small black dot in one corner. No-one said that they saw the large white sheet.

That is how human nature is – blind to the good that there is in others. We only see their black dots.

This is only due to pride. Humble people never have any difficulty in being thankful to God for their fellow-believers. It is only Satanic pride that makes people unthankful for their brothers and sisters.

What good and wonderful brothers and sisters God has given us in the church! And we have been so foolish as to not recognize their worth. Let us learn to thank God for our brothers and sisters at least now.

If we can get some light on ourselves even by reading an article like this, can you imagine how much more light we will get on our selfishness and pride, when the bright light of heaven shines on us, at Jesus' return?

Esau did not find an opportunity for repentance "afterwards", even though he shed many tears then (*Hebrews 12:17*).

There will be an "afterwards" in all of our lives, when we stand before the Lord. In that day, we will discover that it is too late to learn to be thankful. It will be too late to weep then. Now is the time to judge ourselves and to mourn and weep, if we want to have no regret then.

Let us ask God then to give us a fresh revelation of the glory of Jesus. In that light, we will see the depths of selfishness, stubbornness, self-will and pride within our own flesh. And we will fall on our faces before Him in repentance and sorrow. Then it will be easy to finish totally with judging and criticising others.

Let us not be satisfied with purifying ourselves until we reach "Jesus' standard of purity" (*1 John 3:3*). If that is our goal, then we will not have to shrink away in shame when the Lord returns.

17

The Influence of One Man

"I searched for ONE MAN among them who should build up the wall and stand before Me…but I did not find even one man" (Ezekiel 22:30).

God has many tasks to accomplish in this world, and all of them are not of equal importance. For the unimportant tasks, He may use anyone. But for the really important tasks, any man will not do. For such vital tasks, God has to have a man who has been tested and proved through many trials and testings. And if such a man is not immediately available, then God will wait until such a man IS available. God does not do His work with the best available person, as men do.

We use a matchstick to light a fire. But then we throw the matchstick away, because it is no longer of any value to us. There are some people whom God uses like that. He discards them, after He has used them, because they are not valuable to Him. We should never therefore desire to be merely USED by God. We should seek to be valuable to Him.

"In a large house there are not only gold and silver vessels, but also vessels of wood and of earthenware, some to honour and some to dishonour. If a man cleanses himself, he will be a vessel for honour, sanctified, useful to the Master" (*2 Timothy 2:20, 21*).

A man may use vessels of different materials in his work. But he will not value the earthen pots and the wooden crates as much as he values the gold and silver vessels. In the same way, although all who are born again may be equally children of God, every child of God is NOT equally useful to Him in His work. Although there is no partiality with God, yet every vessel is not a sanctified, useful vessel. God prizes only very few, because they alone seek His will and His glory wholeheartedly.

This is why we must cleanse ourselves constantly from "all filthiness of the flesh and spirit" (in other words, from everything that is unlike Christ within us), if we are to be valuable vessels to God (*2 Corinthians 7:1*).

Once a person becomes a valuable vessel, God will depend on him greatly for His work. If such a man fails God, God's work will be halted temporarily, until God can find another man whom He can use.

In the history of the world, of Israel and of the church, we see a number of examples of how God has very often been dependent on just ONE man in a particular situation to accomplish His purposes. But one man with God is always a majority.

Noah

When the whole world was filled with wickedness and rebellion against God, in Noah's time, although there were eight God-fearing people on the earth, yet the fulfillment of God's purposes depended entirely on the faithfulness of just one man, Noah.

Noah was the only man who found favour in God's eyes at that time (*Genesis 6:8*). If that one man had been unfaithful to God, the entire human race would have been wiped out, and none of us would have been alive today!! We can certainly thank God that Noah remained faithful.

Jesus said that the last days would be like the days of Noah. The sexual perversion and violence of the days of Noah would characterise the last days too. This is the time that we are living in today. And so, uncompromising men like Noah are what God needs even today.

Moses

When the Israelites were in Egypt, God could not set them free from their slavery until He had found a man who was fit to represent Him. And God was prepared to wait till such a man was ready.

God's had planned for the Israelites to be in Egypt for 400 years (*Genesis 15:13*). But they finally stayed for 430 years (*Exodus 12:40*). Why did they have to stay 30 years longer than God's perfect plan for them?

It was certainly not because God made a mistake. God never makes any mistakes. But the man who was to be their leader was not yet ready. God had probably planned for Moses to be ready within ten years of his going into the wilderness. But instead Moses took forty years to complete his spiritual education there, under God's hand. So the Israelites had to remain in slavery for another 30 years.

Once when Moses was away from the Israelites for just 40 days, all 2 million of them went astray (*Exodus 32*). It took just a few days for a whole nation to forsake the true God and to go astray worshipping idols, once God's man was away from the scene. Those Israelites had seen amazing miracles before their very eyes. But the memory of those miracles could not preserve the Israelites from worshipping idols. Only the strict leadership of one man of God could do that!

Aaron was their temporary leader, while Moses was away on the mountain. But although Aaron may have been a good, God-fearing man, he could not keep the people devoted to God. Obviously he was a man who sought to please the masses, and the people took advantage of him.

There are many Christian leaders like Aaron today, who imagine themselves to be serving the Lord. They are good, upright people, who live God-fearing lives. But God cannot use them to keep His church pure, because they yield to the will of the people easily. God looks for men like Moses, even today, to lead His church in its battle against Satan.

Joshua

Joshua was another man whom the Lord exalted and stood by. The Lord told Joshua when Israel reached the border of Canaan, "This day I will begin to exalt you in the sight of all Israel, that they may know that just as I have been with Moses, I will be with you" (*Joshua 3:7*).

The Lord had already trained Joshua, for 40 years during the wilderness journey. Now He exalted him to leadership and stood by him just like He had stood by Moses. The Lord even stopped the earth from rotating on its own axis for a number of hours once, to support Joshua. The Bible says that "there was no day like that before it or after it, when the Lord listened to the voice of a man" (*Joshua 10:14*).

Once God has chosen a man to represent Him, it is amazing what miracles He will do to manifest to others that He stands by him.

We read that the Israelites "served the Lord all the days of Joshua, and all the days of the elders who survived Joshua" (*Judges 2:7*).

Joshua's influence was so powerful on the Israelites that they did not dare to worship idols during his lifetime and during the lifetime of his fellow-elders. But once Joshua died, Israel backslid badly.

Such is the effect of the life of one man of God.

Elijah

Consider another time in Israel's history, when Ahab made everyone worship Baal. There were 7000 men at that time in Israel, who refused to worship Baal (*1 Kings 19:18*). That was undoubtedly a bold and creditable stand to take. But such a testimony was still a negative one: They did NOT worship idols. This is like the negative testimony that many believers have today – they do not smoke, they do not gamble, etc.

But God could not use even one of these 7000 men to accomplish His purposes in Israel at that time. For that, God needed an Elijah. Ahab was not afraid of these 7000 "believers". But he was afraid of Elijah. These 7000 men no doubt prayed to God; but their prayers could not bring fire down from heaven. It was the prayer of Elijah, that did that.

The prayers of all believers are not equal in their effect in God's presence. The Bible says in relation to Elijah, that "the effective prayer of a righteous man can accomplish much." (*James 5:17, 16*).

One man single-handedly, turned a whole nation back to God, routed the forces of wickedness and killed all the prophets of Baal.

It is through one faithful man, and not through a multitude, that God's purposes are accomplished, even today.

Elisha

There were fifty "sons of the prophets" (Bible-school students) in Elijah's time who were all hoping to be prophets in Israel one day. But the Spirit of God bypassed all of them and came upon Elisha, who was not a "son of a prophet" (*2 Kings 2:7, 15*). Elisha was known in Israel only as a servant – "one who used to pour water on Elijah's hands" (*2 Kings 3:11*).

When the army of the king of Aram attacked Israel, none of these fifty Bible-scholars could protect Israel – for although they may have studied the Law of Moses in their Bible-school, they did not know God. Only Elisha, who was the only man in Israel who was in touch with God, could forewarn the nation as to where exactly the enemy would attack.

Today also, the main function of a prophet is similar: To warn God's people in advance of where Satan will attack them. One prophet like Elisha, in a church today, can save God's people from spiritual calamity more than fifty preachers ("sons of the prophets"). Bible-knowledge is of no use if a man cannot hear the Spirit's voice. Only a man who can hear God's voice can save a church from Satan's schemes and attacks.

The prophets of old were also called "SEERS" ("those who can SEE into the future with God-given vision" – *1 Samuel 9:9*). They knew where the enemy would attack, and could foresee the dangers of taking a particular course of action. The church today greatly needs such seers.

Daniel

When God wanted to bring the Israelites out of Egypt into Canaan. He needed a man. He found Moses. When He wanted to bring the Jews out of Babylon into Jerusalem, He needed another man. He found Daniel.

The length of the captivity in Babylon (70 years) had been predicted just like the length of the captivity in Egypt had been predicted. But this time(unlike as in Moses' time), there wasn't a delay of even a single day in God's plan being fulfilled – because God's man was ready on time.

Daniel had been faithful from his youth and had passed every test with flying colours. As a young teenager in Babylon, he took a firm stand for the Lord. "He determined in his heart that he would not defile himself" (*Daniel 1:8*) – a good verse for all young people to remember.

Whereas all the other young Jews readily ate the food served on the king's table for fear of the king (food that God had forbidden in Leviticus), Daniel alone refused to eat it. There were three other young men at that table that day, who saw Daniel take a stand, and joined him. Daniel and those three men then became a powerful influence for God in Babylon.

70 years later, when Daniel was nearly 90 years old, his prayers triggered the movement of the Jews from Babylon back to Jerusalem.

Today also there is a movement of God's people from spiritual Babylon (the false church) towards spiritual Jerusalem (the Body of Christ). And for such a movement too God needs men.

There are many today, who are like Daniel's three friends, Hananiah, Mishael and Azariah (*Daniel 1:11*). They are eager to stand for the Lord, but they don't have the courage to do so on their own. They are waiting for a Daniel to lead them. And so God is again looking for Daniels.

Paul

Under the new covenant, God desires to use ALL His children – and not just one man here and there. This is possible however, only if every believer lives in the new-covenant. But right from the days of the apostles, we see that very few believers enter the new covenant. Most believers live lives defeated by sin, are occupied with a "health-and-wealth gospel", need a pastor as a mediator between them and Christ, etc., etc. They still live in many ways exactly like the Old Testament Israelites.

And therefore, just as in Old Testament times, God is again dependent on one man in many a situation, to keep Satan out of His church.

Consider what happened in Ephesus: Paul spent more time there than in any other church. Every single day, for 3 years, he preached the whole counsel of God there (*Acts 20:31*). It was the most privileged of all the churches. The high standard of the teachings in Paul's letter to them indicates that it was a spiritually-minded church too. So, if there was one church where believers should have entered in great numbers into new-covenant life, it should have been this church at Ephesus. But alas, it was not so. Not even the elders there had entered into such a life.

> Paul told those elders when he was leaving them, "I know that after my departure, savage wolves will come in among you, not sparing the flock; and from among your own selves men will arise, speaking perverse things, to draw away the disciples after them" (*Acts 20:29, 30*).

As long as Paul was personally present in the church at Ephesus, no wolf could enter it, because Paul was a watchful shepherd of the flock and a strict doorkeeper of the Lord's house. The elders who were seeking their own, also could not draw away any disciples after them, as long as Paul was there – because they were powerless in Paul's presence.

Paul knew the spiritual condition of the elders. And so he knew that as soon as he left Ephesus, the church would be overrun by the wolves and self-seeking elders – and the testimony would be corrupted. When we read the Second Letter to the Ephesians (*Revelation 2:1–7*), we see that the church there did backslide, exactly as Paul had predicted.

> Who then had preserved the church in Ephesus in purity during those three years? JUST ONE MAN – PAUL. Satan was afraid of Paul, but he knew he could handle all the other elders in Ephesus quite easily!

This has also been the history of every single group that God has raised up anywhere in the world, during the last 20 centuries.

When we look back at the history of the church during the last 20 centuries what do we see? At a particular time, in a particular place, God raises up a man to restore to the church, truths from His Word that had lain buried for ages. God trains such a man in secret, and then brings him forth into a public ministry. Most believers hate this man and call him a heretic and reject him as a false prophet. But a few, who have ears to hear the truth, recognise God's anointing on him, realise that what he is saying is the truth of God, and join him. Thus through these few, a testimony is raised up for the Lord, in that generation. Things go well as long as the man himself is alive. But once he is dead, things begin to decline, and very soon this new group also drifts and soon becomes a part of Babylon, like all the other denominations.

Not a single leader in the history of Christianity has been able to produce a second generation of leaders who have had the same knowledge of God that he himself had. Each of them could serve only their own generation and pass on. In the next generation, God has always had to make a fresh beginning to raise up a pure testimony for His Name.

This is what has happened time and again throughout church history – whether we consider the history of the larger denominations or the smaller groups.

Today, even though all these groups may still proclaim the same doctrines that their founders proclaimed, yet every single one of them has drifted away from the knowledge and life of God that their founders had. They have ALL fallen over either the one cliff of worldliness and compromise, or the opposite cliff of Pharisaism and legalism.

But God needs a pure testimony for His Name in EVERY generation. And He will not leave Himself without a witness even in our generation. Will you pay the price to be wholly available to God in this generation?

18

Learning Gentleness from Jesus

"Learn from Me, for I am gentle and humble in heart" (Matthew 11:29).

Jesus told us to learn two things from Him – humility and gentleness. Generally speaking, many have spoken and written about the humility of Christ. But not much is written or spoken about the gentleness of Christ. This has led to an imbalance in the personal lives of many believers and also in the church.

We see Christ's severity in the way He rebuked the Pharisees (*Matthew 23*) and Peter (*Matthew 16:23*), and in the way He turned over the tables of the money changers and drove them out of the temple (*John 2:14–16*). That represented one aspect of God's nature that Jesus manifested.

But we also see the gentleness of God in the way Jesus dealt with notorious sinners.

We see something of the gentleness of Jesus in the way He spoke to the woman of Samaria, for example. Jesus had asked her about her husband. The woman immediately changed the subject and asked Jesus a totally unrelated question about worship (*John 4:17–24*). And we see there that Jesus did not press the issue of her immoral past, but allowed her to change the subject, and answered her question about worship.

If we embarrass another person by probing curiously into details about their past life, or by repeating things that touch sore points in their life, we can be certain that we have learnt NOTHING of the gentleness of Christ from the Holy Spirit.

Curiosity is a sin that even many believers have not recognised as a demonic vice. Our flesh has a great longing to know about the evils that others have done, and so will always be desirous of listening to the sins of others, even when they are shared under the pretext of being prayer-requests. Such information however will never do us any good, but on the contrary will pollute our minds, prejudice us against others, make us evil,

162

and hinder our witness and our ministry for the Lord. That is how Satan leads many believers astray.

We must never allow others to tell us about their past lives even voluntarily, for man must confess his sins only to God, not to other men.

Sin must be confessed only in the circle in which it was committed.

Sins of the thought-life and those committed in private that hurt no-one but ourselves, must be confessed ONLY to God. But sins that hurt another person, must be confessed to God as well as to that other person. Sins committed against a local body of believers must be confessed to God as well as publicly in the assembly meeting.

A gentle person will always be cautious never to say anything that will probe curiously into the private areas of another's life or into his past. If we accidentally touch someone at a sore point, and see the person's discomfiture, we should be quick to change the subject and act as though we know nothing. That is gentleness.

We see the gentleness of Jesus also in the way He dealt with the woman caught in adultery (*John 8:1–12*). Jesus certainly did not condone her sin or call her sin by some other name. He called her adultery 'sin' and told her very clearly that she must not commit sin again. But He did not throw stones at her for being sinful.

God does not throw stones at sinners. We must never forget that.

There are two ways to preach about victory over sin. One is the way Jesus preached it, without throwing stones at people. The other is the way the Pharisees preached it, by condemning people.

The gentleness of Christ is missing in the words of many who preach on victory over sin. They tell others not to sin, but they also criticise them, accuse them and refer to them by hard names. The Pharisees were like that. They preached about righteousness, but they considered everyone "accursed" who did not belong to their group (*John 7:49*). We find the same attitude in many believers today.

Jesus on the other hand, preached a much higher standard of righteousness than the Pharisees ever did. But He never called any sinner by bad names. He loved them and won them to a godly life, through His gentleness.

The woman caught in adultery realized that while the Pharisees had come only to point out her sin and to accuse her and expose her, Jesus wanted to save her. And she must certainly have been saved and become one of Jesus' disciples, after that encounter with Him.

When Jesus preached to that sinful woman, He did not preach doctrine to her, but encouragement. He came with a message of salvation from the power of sin, and not just with a doctrine on holiness.

A lot of today's "holiness-preaching" however majors on doctrines that define the old man and the flesh, and the new and living way through the flesh etc. But rarely do we see the gentleness of Jesus in those who preach these profound truths. And so sinners are not attracted to such Pharisees, as they were attracted to Jesus.

This is where all of us who preach holiness would do well to examine our own lives and see how our message comes across to others. Is the gentleness of Christ present in our ministry?

Christ must be manifest in our flesh, if others are to be drawn to Him. We must allow the Holy Spirit to show us the gentleness of Jesus, and to transform us into that likeness if we are to fulfil our ministry.

Do you throw stones at others? Do you point an accusing finger at another? If so, then you are more like the Devil than like God. For it is Satan who accuses. God never accuses. The Bible tells us very clearly, "God will love you and not accuse you" (*Zephaniah 3:17* - TLB).

The Bible says that judgment is "an unusual and extraordinary work" of God (*Isaiah 28:21*). That is not what God does normally or usually. With man however it is different. Judging others is his normal work. This is where it becomes clear that man has been infected by Satan's poison.

It is easy to deceive ourselves that we are growing into the likeness of Christ, when we are not. If we haven't got rid of the habit of accusing and judging others, we are certainly not growing in Christlikeness.

The Bible says that we should not seek to be teachers (*James 3:1*).

What do teachers normally do? When they come home from school each day, with all the books of their students, they correct and correct and correct.... That is what they do, day after day, and year after year.

We are not to be like those teachers, going around correcting others and giving them marks, day after day. Those who do so are warned in that same verse that they will be judged more severely.

If we are gentle, we will make allowance for the failures of others, and believe that there could be hidden factors that we are unaware of, that may have caused them to fail.

Suppose you came home from work one evening, and saw that your son had done a sum wrong in his homework, and scolded him severely for it. And then if your wife showed you 10 sheets of paper in which your son had tried to do that very sum for one hour before you came in, how would you feel? Wouldn't you regret having been so hard on your son?

That is how it is when we judge others. We do not know, for example, how much a person had resisted a sin before he actually fell into it. We only see the person's fall and judge by what we see. But God sees the hours in which that person struggled and fought to avoid falling, and judges more mercifully than we do.

Ephesians 4:2 reads, "Be gentle. Be patient with each other, making allowance for each other's faults because of your love (TLB)."

In the book of Job, we see an example of God's gentleness. There we read how Job complained and murmured against God during his sickness (*Job 3 to 31*). His words were full of unbelief and bitterness, and he should have been judged severely by God. But God loved Job and made allowance for him. He knew that Job was under much pressure, because he had lost all his property and his ten children in one day, had become sick with an incurable sickness, and on top of it all, was also being accused by his wife.

Further, Job was living at a time when "overcoming grace" was not available – unlike today. And so God spoke gently to Job and did not hold his words against him. God knew the background situation and so He was gentle. We usually never know anything of the background situation. And so we are hard. That is why the Bible tells us not to judge.

In *Isaiah 61:2*, we read that the Lord Jesus was anointed to proclaim "the favourable year (365 days) of the Lord and the day (1 day) of vengeance of God".

We know from *Romans 11:22* that God is both kind and severe – but it is only in *Isaiah 61*, that we read that the proportion of God's kindness to His severity is not 50:50 but 365:1!!

That gentle nature is what we are called to partake of.

Jesus told His disciples that only those who are merciful to others would receive mercy from God (*Matthew 5:7*).

Mercy in the New Testament means more than just forgiving others who have harmed us.

In *Luke 10:25–37*, at the end of the parable of the good Samaritan, the actions of the Samaritan are referred to as his "having shown mercy" to the needy man (*verse 37*). So we see that mercy also means showing kindness to the needy ones who come across our path.

The Bible warns us that, "there will be no mercy to those who have shown no mercy", but encourages us by telling us that "if you have been merciful, then God's mercy toward you will win out over His judgment against you" (*James 2:13*).

In the light of that verse, let us consider how it will be in the day of judgment for two believers – one who was merciful to others and one who was not.

Brother A comes first and stands before the Lord. He was a sincere believer on earth, but one who had not got full victory in many areas. But he was one who fully forgave everyone who did him any harm, and showed kindness to needy people around him. The Lord will look at him and say, "Well, A, there are a number of things in your life that deserve punishment. But I see that you were constantly merciful and gentle to everyone who came across your path. So, I'll treat you just as you treated those others. You can go – free. There is no judgment for you."

Then comes Brother B, who was one who had victory over sin in all conscious areas of his life. He thinks to himself that if Brother A, who was much worse than him, got off so lightly, then he himself would certainly receive a high commendation from the Lord. But B was a brother who was hard and unmerciful on other believers who did not have victory over sin, and constantly referred to them as part of the "harlot" and not a part of Christ's Bride (as though God had given Brother B the task of selecting a bride for His Son!!). Brother B also looked down on believers in other groups and felt that only those who belonged to his own group were God's elect. And now the Lord says to him, "I appreciate the fact that you sought to battle against sin so wholeheartedly. That was good. But you were so hard on other believers and so unmerciful in your judgment of them. So, I'll treat you just as you treated those others. You have to be judged – severely."

What a surprise B will get when he hears those words from the Lord. Many who are first here will be last there.

There was no partiality there in the Lord's treatment of A and B. To both the Lord said exactly the same words: "I'll treat you just as you treated those others." And they both got exactly what they deserved.

This is not an imaginary scene that I have portrayed, but something that we are going to see most certainly when Christ returns – for God's Word can never lie.

Read *James 2:13* again if you still have any doubt about it.

Year after year goes by in the lives of many believers without their ever getting rid of this Satanic habit of being hard on others and judging them unmercifully. Let us determine that this year will be different.

Let us ask God for His grace and for the power of His Spirit to finish with all judgment of others this year, to finish with all curiosity into the private lives and affairs of others, to finish with all being busybodies in the matters of others, to finish with all criticism of other brothers and their wives and children.

Let us instead pursue increasingly the path of partaking of the gentleness of Christ. Then we shall not have lived this year in vain.

19

Your Decisions Determine What You Become

"I came down from heaven, not to do My own will, but the will of Him Who sent Me" (John 6:38).

Jesus tells us here in His own words what He came on earth to do. And in this one sentence we have a description of how Jesus lived every single day of His entire life on earth.

The thirty years of Jesus' life in Nazareth are referred to as hidden years. But here Jesus reveals what He did during every day of those 30 years: He denied His own will and He did His Father's will.

When Jesus was with the Father in heaven from eternity past, He never had to deny His own will, for His own will was the same as His Father's. But when He came to earth in our flesh, that flesh had a self-will that was diametrically opposed to the Father's will at every single point. The only way in which Jesus could do His Father's will then was by denying His own self-will all the time. This was the cross that Jesus bore throughout His earthly life – the crucifixion of His own will – and which He now asks us to bear every day, if we are to follow Him.

It was the consistent denial of His own will that made Jesus a spiritual Man. And it is the denial of our self-will that will make us spiritual too.

Every day we make decisions concerning various matters. We make decisions in relation to how we are going to spend our money or our spare time, or how to speak to, or about someone, or how to write a particular letter, or how to react to another's behaviour, or how much time to spend in studying the Word or in prayer or in serving the church etc. We react to the actions and words and behaviour of people around us from morning till night. We may not be realising it, but we make at least a hundred decisions every day – and in each of those decisions we decide either to please ourselves or to please God.

Many of our actions are not the result of conscious decisions. But even then, we do them in one of these two ways – either seeking to please ourselves or to glorify God. Our unconscious actions are determined by the way we make our conscious decisions. Finally, it is the sum total of these decisions that determine whether we become spiritual or carnal.

Think of the millions of decisions that we have made ever since we were first converted. Those who have consciously and consistently chosen to deny their self-will many times each day and to do the will of God, have become spiritual. On the other hand, those who have rejoiced merely in the forgiveness of their sins, and who therefore chose to please themselves most of the time have remained carnal. Each person's decisions have determined what he has finally become.

You are today as humble and as holy and as loving as you yourself have chosen to be, through the thousands of decisions that you have made in the various situations of life in past years.

Spirituality is not something that comes through one encounter with God. It is the result of choosing the way of self-denial and of doing God's will CONSISTENTLY day after day, week after week, and year after year.

Consider the spiritual state of two brothers (both converted to Christ on the same day), ten years after their conversion. One is now a mature brother with spiritual discernment, to whom God can commit much responsibility in the church. The other is still a child, without discernment, and needing to be fed and encouraged by others constantly.

What is it that has made such a difference between the two?

The answer is: The little decisions that they took during each day of the ten years of their Christian life.

If they continue on in the same way, in another 10 years, the difference between them will be even more pronounced. And in eternity, their differing degrees of glory will be as different as the light emitted by a 2000-watt bulb and a 5-watt bulb!!

"One star differs from another star in glory" (*1 Corinthians 15:41*).

Consider a situation where you are visiting a home and you are tempted to say something negative about a certain brother (whom you don't like) who is not present. What do you do? Will you yield to that temptation and backbite, or will you deny yourself and keep your mouth shut? Nobody ever gets struck down by God with leprosy or cancer just because they spoke evil of someone. No. And therefore many imagine that such a sin will not destroy their lives. Alas, it is only in eternity that many brothers and sisters will realise how every time they pleased themselves, they destroyed themselves a little. Then they will regret the way they wasted their lives on earth.

Jesus too was tempted in similar situations for 30 years in Nazareth. It is written about those hidden years that "He never pleased Himself" at any time (*Romans 15:3*). He always denied Himself. Thus He pleased the Father at all times.

Pleasing oneself can be done in many areas of one's life – for example, in the area of eating. Consider a situation where, even when you are not hungry, you decide to spend some money to buy some tasty snacks to eat. There is certainly nothing sinful or wrong in that. But it speaks of a certain way of life. Because you have money, you buy what you like, whether you need it or not. You do what pleases yourself. If you feel like buying something you buy it. If you feel like going somewhere, you go. If you feel like sleeping late, you just sleep late. What is the end result of living like that, even if you go regularly to the meetings and read your Bible every day? You may not lose your salvation, but you will certainly waste the one life that God gave you to live for Him.

Another brother however acts differently. He decides to discipline his body. When he is not hungry, he decides not to eat anything unnecessarily. He decides never to buy any unnecessary things for himself. He decides to get up 15 minutes earlier each day to spend time with God. When someone speaks to him angrily, he decides to reply gently. He decides to remain in love and goodness always. He decides not to read certain news items in the newspapers that will stimulate his lusts. In every situation, he decides to humble himself and not to justify himself. He decides to give up certain friendships that are influencing him towards the world. Through constantly deciding to deny his own will (what pleased him), he becomes strong in his will to please God alone.

What did he lose by not buying that unnecessary thing, or by getting out of bed 15 minutes earlier, or by giving up his human sense of dignity and asking for forgiveness? Nothing. But think of what he has gained!

A man like that, who is consistently faithful in the little things will in a few years' time become a trustworthy man of God – not because of the Bible-knowledge that he possesses, but because of his faithfulness in the little decisions he takes in life not to please Himself but to please God.

Don't be weak-willed then. Exercise your will to please God at all times. Mature Christians are those who "because of practice (in exercising their will in the right direction through many years), have their senses trained to discern good and evil" (*Hebrews 5:14*).

Consider an illustration: Two fat men go to a doctor to remove their flabbiness. The doctor gives them a course of exercises for the next twelve months. One man goes through the discipline of those exercises consistently every day, and slims down and becomes strong. The other man does the exercises for the first few days and then slackens off and finally gives up altogether. His pot-belly gets fatter and fatter with his indisciplined ways, until he finally dies prematurely. This is an illustration of how we can either make our wills strong to do God's will, or leave them flabby and weak for the devil to exploit.

I remember reading once of a young servant of the Lord who felt that he had been watching too much television (even though he had been watching only clean programs), and who decided one day not only to sell his TV set, but also to use the time that he had spent watching TV, in prayer every day. As a direct result of that little decision that he took – and maintained – God gave him a ministry that blessed thousands.

Those who see nothing wrong in watching clean programs over TV, find that God does not entrust them with much – for He is a rewarder of those who diligently seek Him and there is no partiality with Him.

Yes, you are what you are today because of those many, many little decisions that you have taken in relation to either denying yourself or pleasing yourself in the areas of food, money, sleep, reading, etc.

Time is running out fast. Those who are over 40 years of age, and who have spent their lives pleasing themselves, cannot expect to do much for God now, for they have wasted the best years of their lives. Those past years of your life are gone – gone forever. Even Almighty God cannot restore them to you. But if you repent even now, you may yet be able to do something useful for God with the second half of your life.

But I want to speak primarily to those who are still in their teenage years and in their twenties: Let me tell you that God wants to bless you in such a way that you become a blessing to others. He wants to entrust an important ministry in His church to you by the time you are 30 or 35 years old. But will He find you faithful in the next ten years or so of your life, so that He can accomplish His will in your life?

If you determine to be faithful from now on, you will have no regrets in eternity, no matter how much you may have failed in your past life up until now. Take life seriously then. Think of how Jesus lived in the days of His flesh in Nazareth, and follow His example. Say to yourself, "I have been born on this earth, to DENY my own will, and to DO the will of my Heavenly Father"

Do you think the devil will allow you take seriously what I am telling you now? No. He will tell you that there is plenty of time. He will tell you that such a life of self-denial will be a strain. He will tell you that God doesn't mind your enjoying yourself, or indulging yourself a little bit here and there. He will tell you to take it easy etc., etc. Why? Because he wants you to drift aimlessly for the next twenty years, and to wake up when it is too late. Young people, don't be fooled by Satan. God has given you only one life, and time is running out fast. Don't waste it.

You will find more than enough believers around you (even among those who have understood the new and living way) who have no interest in living such a disciplined, wholehearted life. Don't judge them. Don't be a Pharisee and despise them. Mind your own business and don't be a busybody in their affairs. Believe the best about them and leave them alone. But at the same time don't follow their example. Be different. Let Jesus alone be your Example. You have a calling over your life and you cannot afford to lose that, no matter what else you may lose on this earth. Think often of the day when you will have to give an account of your life at the judgment-seat of Christ.

> So forget the blunders that you have made in life. Repent radically of your sins and be wholehearted in the days to come. God forgives you and blots out your past. Don't mope over your failures now, or you will be a drifter in the future too. The memory of your failures will help you to recognise that you are what you are only by the grace of God. It will also enable you to keep your face in the dust at all times before God.

Determine that you will become a true man/woman of God.

20

Satan is the Ruler of Darkness and the Father of Lies

Satan is called "the ruler of darkness" and "the father of lies" (*Ephesians 6:12; John 8:44*). Both these titles are descriptive of his character and his ministry.

All that constitutes spiritual darkness in this universe is a territory that has been allotted by God to Satan. All those who wander into this territory (whether believers or unbelievers) can expect the ruler of darkness to get a foothold in their lives. Whenever we do anything that cannot stand the light of God, we open ourselves to Satan. Our safety is in the light. Only there does the blood of Jesus cleanse us from all sin, and only there can we have fellowship with the Father (*1 John 1:9*). Satan knows this, and that is why he constantly urges believers to do things that cannot stand the light of God. It is thus that even Spirit-filled believers lose their anointing.

All lying originates from Satan too. All who give room to any type of lying or deception or hypocrisy in their lives – whether believers or unbelievers – allow Satan thereby to make an inroad into their lives. Satan knows this, and that is why he encourages believers everywhere to live before the face of men, for that is the surest way to be a hypocrite. Hypocrisy is falsehood and is fathered by Satan.

We cannot overcome Satan if we do not first cleanse ourselves from anything that gives him a foothold in our lives. The Bible commands us to "submit to God" first, and then to "resist the Devil" (*James 4:7*).

This is why we should make a careful evaluation of our lives and see where we have given room to Satan by walking in darkness or in guile.

Before Jesus went to the cross, He said, "The ruler of the world is coming, and he has nothing in Me." (*John 14:30*). Satan could find no lying, guile or darkness in Jesus.

We too can keep ourselves in such a way, that the evil one is not able to get any foothold at any time in our lives. "He who is born of God keeps himself and the evil one does not touch him" (*1 John 5:18*).

21

Helping God!!

We can create a lot of confusion in God's work and in our own lives when we use our human reasoning and try to help God according to our own understanding.

"The Lord said to Abraham, 'Look towards the heavens, and count the stars. So shall your descendants be.' ... Now Sarah had borne Abraham no children ... So Sarah took Hagar, the Egyptian, her maid, and gave her to Abraham as his wife ... And Hagar bore Ishmael to him ... And Abraham said to God, 'Oh that Ishmael might live before Thee'. But God said, 'No, but Sarah your wife shall bear you a son ... and I shall establish My covenant with him'" (*Genesis 15:5; 16:1, 3, 16; 17:18, 19*).

God had promised Abraham seed as countless as the stars. Yet Sarah was barren. Abraham and Sarah must have both feared that God's Name would be dishonoured, if the promise was not fulfilled. So at Sarah's suggestion, Abraham took another wife and had a son through her, in order to help God out of a tight spot!!

What Abraham did not realise was that God needs no such help. The help that he offered God (by producing Ishmael) finally caused problems not only for his wife, but also for his son Isaac and his descendants.

How often we feel that without our help, God's promises will not be fulfilled. And so we move and act when God hasn't told us to move or act. We trust in our man-made plans and efforts to do God's work, and don't believe sufficiently in waiting on the Lord to direct us.

Jesus never did anything in His life without seeking His Father's will and guidance (*John 5:19, 30*). But most believers don't seek God's will and guidance like that, because they trust more in themselves than in God!!

Our lack of prayer and our leaning on our own understanding (or our wife's understanding, as in Abraham's case above!!!) in the decisions that we take, is what brings confusion in our homes, and in God's work.

"The Lord said to Moses, 'Speak to the rock that it may yield its water'.... Then Moses lifted up his hand and struck the rock twice with his rod.... And the Lord said to Moses, 'Because you have not believed Me, you shall not bring this assembly into the land" (Numbers 20:7–13).

God had asked Moses only to speak to the rock this time. But Moses decided to help God by striking the rock twice. How true it is that the flesh would rather strike hard (and twice) than speak gently (once)! We feel that God's purposes will be accomplished quicker with a bit of human hardness, even when He commands us to be gentle (*Matthew 11:28*). But it is through His kindness that God leads people to repentance (*Romans 2:4*).

Moses may also have felt that since God had asked him to strike the rock once before (*Exodus 17:6*), it must be so every time. Many imagine that the Holy Spirit must always work in the same way as He did earlier or elsewhere! And so they try to help Him with psychological gimmicks to bring "revival", to "heal" the sick, and to get people to "speak in tongues". What they don't realise is that the Holy Spirit works differently at different times, and does not need any soulish help to manifest his gifts.

"Uzzah reached out toward the ark of God and took hold of it, for the oxen nearly upset it. And the anger of the Lord burned against Uzzah, and God struck him down there for his irreverence; and he died there" (2 Samuel 6:6, 7).

Uzzah's intentions were good. He really longed to protect the ark of God's testimony from falling down. But he was not a Levite, and so he had no right to touch the ark. He went outside his boundaries. This was so serious a matter, that God slew him. We cannot trifle with God's laws.

In the church too, God has given different responsibilities to different ones and drawn boundaries around each one. When we see a lack in a certain area and seek to help God by trying to resolve the problem, we need to first ask ourselves whether the

Spirit is leading us to do that, or whether it is our own human reasoning that is urging us to do something about it. God respects everyone's boundaries, even if we don't. And God does not need any help from us, outside the boundaries that he has drawn around us. Only within those boundaries can we find God (*Acts 17:26, 27*). Outside them, we will find only the Devil (*Ecclesiastes 10:8b*).

The application to our lives, of the principles outlined in the above examples, are manifold. Let us ask God then for light on this matter in relation to our own life and ministry.

22

The Ministry of Melchizedek

"Thou art a Priest forever after the order of Melchizedek"
(Hebrews 7:17).

Melchizedek was an unknown man – but a man who knew God intimately – who met Abraham when Abraham was returning from a war, and blessed him with food, and with a word from God (*Genesis 14:14–20*).

Abraham was tired and was in great danger of being puffed up after being so victorious. He was also in danger of coveting the property of the king of Sodom that he had captured in the war. But God sent Melchizedek with food that refreshed his tired body, and with a word that saved his soul from being defiled by pride and covetousness.

Melchizedek told Abraham, "Blessed be God, the Possessor of heaven and earth Who gave you the victory over your enemies." He did not preach a long 7-point sermon to him. No. He just spoke one sentence – but that was a prophetic word that met Abraham's need exactly.

Through that one sentence, he reminded Abraham that since it was God Who had given him the victory, he should not take the credit to himself. He also reminded Abraham that since his God owned the heaven and earth, there was no need for him to take any of the spoils of the battle, as victors normally do.

A few minutes later, when Abraham met the king of Sodom, these words of Melchizedek helped him to do the right thing. He told the king of Sodom that since his God was the Possessor of heaven and earth, he would not take even a thread from the spoils (*Genesis 14:22–24*).

Jesus has now been appointed by God as a high-priest after the order of Melchizedek. And we are now to be priests according to the same order – and are to fulfil this Melchizedek-ministry.

Consider how Melchizedek, without any show, or pomp, or publicity, or advertisement, appeared quietly and gave Abraham just what he needed – food for his bodily needs, and the right word to save Abraham from pride and covetousness. After meeting Abraham's need, he disappeared just as quietly as he came. This is the ministry that we must all covet – to quietly bless those in need and then to disappear without seeking any honour, appreciation, thanks or publicity for ourselves.

People come to the meetings of the church, tired and exhausted from their battles in the world in which they live and work. How wonderful it is to prophesy in the church like Melchizedek, so that the believers are provided with spiritual food and nourishment that can refresh them. How blessed also to be able to help them in practical, earthly ways, when they are in need of it, so that we can make life easier for them.

It is sad when brothers have high thoughts about themselves, and speak for a long time in the meetings of the church with very little content in what they say. Such long, boring sermons bring death into the meeting. How wonderful, on the other hand, to be able to have the right word – a prophetic word – for the brothers and sisters in every meeting.

But if we are to prophesy like this, we must be priests who have offered sacrifices to God in secret, and who keep in touch with God at all times, with a clear conscience.

There is no partiality with God. He desires that every brother and sister in the church be a priest after the order of Melchizedek, and prophesy (See *Acts 2:17, 18; 1 Corinthians 14:31*).

If you are willing to lay your all on the altar of sacrifice as a priest, if you long to prophesy, if you have a real care and concern for the welfare of your brothers and sisters, and if you have no desire for your own reputation or honour, then God will surely put a word in your mouth to meet the needs of the brothers and sisters, in every meeting – even if it be just one sentence.

In the priesthood of Melchizedek, no-one is a special brother. Do not seek then to be known because of the gifts you have. Seek to be a nobody. Be anonymous, if you really want a Melchizedek-ministry.

Let there be no thoughts within you that you are the brother who brought certain souls to Christ, or that you are the brother who casts out demons, or prays for the sick, or that you are the brother who leads the meeting, or who does this or that. Be content to be an ordinary brother without any name, title, honour or reputation.

Bless the others and disappear. Seek to be unknown.

Let us rejoice that we are all equal, even though our ministries and gifts may differ. Jesus once told His disciples not to rejoice that demons were subject to them in His Name. In other words, they were not to rejoice in their ministry, that is, in what they could do or had done. They were to rejoice instead in what God had done for them – writing their names in the book of life (*Luke 10:20*).

Such an attitude lies at the core of all new-covenant ministry.

One characteristic of God's nature is that He hates all display and advertisement. It is written about God in the book of Isaiah, "Truly, Thou art a God Who hides Thyself, O God" (*Isaiah 45:15*). God wants to make us like Himself – partaking of His nature that loves to do things without being noticed, and without wanting any credit for what has been done.

God wants to do such a mighty work in us that we too can learn how to bless the others and then disappear, like Melchizedek did. He wants to free us totally from this Satanic evil of seeking honour and credit from men for what we have done.

May there be many in our midst who are priests after the order of Melchizedek.

23

The Secret of Discernment

"The religious rulers were sneering at Jesus…. The soldiers also mocked Him…. One of the criminals who were hanged there was hurling abuse at Him…. But the other rebuking him said, 'This man has done nothing wrong'" (Luke 22:35–41).

It is indeed amazing that while the elderly Bible-scholars in Israel, and the shrewd, educated Roman soldiers could not discern Who Jesus was, a thief-cum-murderer who knew nothing of the Bible could do so in his last moments on earth. Why was this so?

Discernment does not come through intelligence, Bible-knowledge or experience. It is given by God to those who are sincere of heart.

The thief on the cross teaches us how we can have discernment.

The entire range of bishops, priests and Bible-scholars in Israel were there at the foot of the cross that day accusing Jesus of one thing and another (*Matthew 27:41*). Many of the chief citizens of the nation also, who were passing by, were abusing Jesus mercilessly and accusing Him of saying that He would destroy the temple (a false accusation, since Jesus never ever made such a statement) (*Matthew 27:39*).

Both the thieves were so convinced by these accusations, that they too joined in the tirade against Jesus (*Matthew 27:44*).

But all of a sudden, one of them stopped, and said concerning Jesus, "This man has not committed a single sin" (*Luke 23:41*).

How did he know that? How did he discern that Jesus was the Messiah that He claimed to be? How did he reject all the accusations of the people as false – at a time when no-one took up for Jesus?

After all, "there cannot be smoke without a fire", can there? Going by the worldly wisdom of that proverb, the thief could have thought that there must be some grounds, however small, in Jesus, for all these hundreds of people to accuse Him.

Yet the thief said that Jesus did NOTHING wrong!!

How did the thief become so spiritually-minded as to reject "what his ears heard" (*Isaiah 11:3*)? Because he heard Jesus saying, "Father, forgive them, for they do not know what they are doing." (*Luke 23:34*).

On one hand, the thief saw the unrest, the agitation, the bitterness and the hatred of those Bible-scholars. On the other hand, he saw the forgiving spirit, the absence of self-justification, and the rest that there was in Jesus. Thus he discerned who was right and who was wrong.

In the church too, this is how we are to exercise discernment. When two brothers or sisters have a controversy, if you use this thief's yardstick, you will soon be able to discover who is right and who is wrong.

"The wicked are like the tossing sea, for it cannot be quiet, and its waters toss up refuse and mud. 'There is no peace', says my God, for the wicked'" (Isaiah 57:20, 21).

Those who are wrong in God's eyes are doomed to a life of constant agitation and unrest, in which they will keep on tossing up rubbish and mud from their mouths (gossip, accusations, complaints and abuses) against godly brothers and sisters. When you meet such a brother or sister, you can, without any hesitation, categorise him/her as a wicked person, for that is what God calls him/her in *Isaiah 57:20, 21*. There is no need for further evidence or even to look into the facts of the case. The unrest and agitation in that person are the clearest evidence of all.

In worldly court-cases, the judges sometimes take many years to sift through all the evidence, before arriving at a judgment. And even then they could be wrong. If we have to adopt this method for disputes in the church, then we will have to spend all our life just listening to one side and the other before arriving at a conclusion. And we could still be wrong!

But God has given us a better way: Just check as to who is at rest and who is in unrest. Check as to who refuses to justify himself and who is full of complaints. And you will have the answer straight-away, as to who is righteous and who is not.

The thief on the cross has shown us the secret of discernment.

24

Submission to the Elders of the Church

"Obey your leaders and submit to them" (Hebrews 13:17).

Where you have confidence in your local church-elders, it is easy to submit to them in all matters. But perhaps you do not have confidence in your elders. Then you must distinguish between church matters and personal matters, so that you know clearly where you have to submit to your elders and where you don't have to.

Church Matters

Church matters include the conduct of the meetings of the church, the spiritual direction the church is going, the emphasis in the ministry of that church, the activities arranged by the church, etc., etc.

In such matters, there must always be total submission to the directions given by the elders. This is not because you respect them as mature brothers, or because you have confidence in them, but just because they are the shepherds in the church in which God has placed you – provided you are sure that God has placed you there.

Jesus submitted to Joseph and Mary, even though they were imperfect and less mature than Him, because His Father had placed Him in their home. That was how He began opening the new and living way through His flesh – in Nazareth during His first 30 years.

We must never forget this fact that the first steps of the new and living way were opened by Jesus through submission to imperfect authorities at home. All the other steps came later.

You must never be the cause of strife in any church – for God hates those who sow discord among the brothers – however spiritual or zealous they may consider themselves to be (*Proverbs 6:16–19*). Rebellion against God-appointed leadership is always

Satanic. It is the way of Korah (*Jude 11; Numbers 16*), and is always the result of pride and arrogance.

If however you are not sure that God has placed you in a particular church, then you must consider before God whether you should leave that church and join another one. But you must never stay in a church and create confusion there, for God will never tolerate that.

> Neither should you be like a visitor in a church, eating the 'food' there as you would in a restaurant, with no sense of responsibility. The church is not a restaurant but a home. So you must commit yourself totally to some local church. Otherwise you will not grow spiritually.

> Remember however, that you will never find an ideal church, for every church is imperfect. But look for a church that is closest to the Word of God – as you understand it at present.

If you feel some time that you should bring in a new emphasis (that is lacking) into a church, then the proper way to do it is by first discussing the issue with the elder brothers, and then to do exactly as they direct. The improper way is to bring in your emphasis in the meetings, by preaching the Word in contradiction to the direction set by the elders.

If you disagree strongly with your elders in any matter, and feel that you cannot submit to their eldership, or if you feel that the elders are leading the church in a wrong direction, then remember that you are always free to leave such a church and start one of your own, with the emphasis that you feel is necessary and important.

If God is with you, He will bless you in your new step – as He blessed Martin Luther, John Wesley, William Booth, Watchman Nee and many others in many lands, through the centuries, who left their original churches and started new ones, under the direction of God.

If however you are acting in your own stubbornness, and God is not with you, you will find yourself following in the footsteps of Theudas and Judas of Galilee (*Acts 5:36, 37*) and many thousands of others in these twenty centuries of Christianity, who started new movements and ended up in confusion and frustration finally.

Personal Matters

Personal matters include matters such as what clothes you wear, how you spend your money, what sort of house you choose to live in, where or how you travel (by air or by train), what clothes you and your family members wear, what food you eat, what toys you buy for your children, whether your children play computer games or not, whether you allow your children to watch sporting events on a neighbour's television or not, what job you take, where you work etc., etc.

In such matters you have perfect freedom to do whatever you feel you should do. You don't have to obey or even consult your elders in such matters, if you don't have confidence in them. If you are in doubt about some such matter, you could even consult an older brother in another place, if you have more confidence in that brother than in your local elders. The final decision in such matters however, is always yours.

There is no rebellion in doing things differently in such matters, unless your elders feel that your conduct or your dress or your children are a stumbling-block to others in the church – in which case, you must be willing to listen to what they have to tell you about it.

The way of wisdom then is to distinguish between where you must submit to the elders in a church, and where you don't have to.

A lack of confidence in your local elders does not mean that you are rebellious – for not all elder brothers are spiritually minded, and not all elder brothers necessarily inspire confidence.

But if you end up submitting to no-one anywhere, then it is easy for you to become a law unto yourself and thus become an easy target for Satan to knock off and destroy.

May God help us all to walk in the way of wisdom at all times.

25

A Spiritual Check-Up

1.   Have I spoken or thought evil of anyone today?
2.   Did I speak any idle words today?
3.   Did I indulge in overeating or laziness or any other filthy lust?
4.   Did I act in a selfish way towards anyone today?
5.   Was I happy or even unconcerned about someone else's failure?
6.   Did I seek the kingdom of God and His righteousness first today?
7.   Did I look for opportunities to witness for Christ and to do good?
8.   Did I doubt the love or the power or the sovereignty of God today?
9.   Was I proud of any accomplishment?
10. Was I discouraged or depressed over anything?
11. Did I do or say anything, which was not profitable or edifying?
12. Did I do to others as I would want them to do to me?
13. Was I carnally inquisitive or a busybody in anyone's affairs?
14. Did I waste money on anything useless today?
15. Did I tell another what was told to me in confidence?
16. Was I impatient with anyone today?
17. How did I treat servants and those on a lower social scale?
18. Did I speak a word of encouragement or appreciation to anyone?
19. Did I show my love to the members of my family?
20. Did I consider myself as better than anyone else?
21. Did I pass judgment on anyone today – even in my thoughts?
22. Is there anyone I have not forgiven totally, from my heart?
23. Did I believe any evil story, without verifying the information?
24. Were my thoughts morally pure today?
25. Have I prayed for those who hate me and persecute me?
26. Was I jealous of anyone today?
27. Did I value and delight in my fellow-believers?

28. Was I concerned about the spiritual & physical needs of my brethren?
29. Is it possible that I might have hurt someone thoughtlessly?
30. Did I keep my word and my promises?
31. Was I a servant to all whom I came across today?
32. Have I cast my every care and burden on the Lord?
33. Was I concerned about the opinion of any man?
34. Did I waste any time today, or did I use the day profitably?
35. Was I alert to hear what the Lord had to say to me today?
36. Did I try to live simply, avoiding luxury as far as possible?
37. Did I share something of spiritual value with my children today?
38. Did I try to help my wife (husband) in her (his) work today?
39. Did I despise anyone who doesn't have the same light as I have?
40. Is there any thought in my heart that is not good, towards anyone?

26

Proving God's Perfect Will

When faced with an issue concerning which we are unsure as to whether it is God's will or not, it is good for us to ask ourselves twelve questions. As we answer these questions honestly, it will become increasingly clear to us what the will of God is.

1. Is it contrary to any of the teachings of Jesus and the apostles, or to the spirit of the New Testament, as far as I know? (*2 Timothy 3:16, 17*)
2. Is it something I can do with a clear conscience? (*1 John 3:21*)
3. Is it something I can do for the glory of God? (*1 Corinthians 10:31*)
4. Is it something I can do in fellowship with Jesus? (*Colossians 3:17*)
5. Can I ask God to bless me as I do it? (*2 Corinthians 9:8*)
6. Will my doing it blunt my spiritual edge in any way? (*2 Timothy 2:15*)
7. Will it be spiritually profitable and edifying, to the best of my knowledge? (*1 Corinthians 6:12; 10:23*)
8. Would I be happy if I were found doing it at the moment when Jesus returns to earth? (*1 John 2:28*)
9. What do wiser and more mature brothers think about it? (*Proverbs 11:14; 15:22; 24:6*)
10. Will my doing it bring dishonour to God's Name or ruin my testimony, if others know about it? (*Romans 2:24; 2 Corinthians 8:21*)
11. Will my doing it cause others to stumble, if they know about it? (*Romans 14:13; 1 Corinthians 8:9*)
12. Do I feel free in my spirit to do it? (*1 John 2:27*)

(Look up the Scripture references and meditate on them).